# NIPSEY HUSSLE BIOGRAPHY

## The Marathon of Greatness

**Christopher Andrew Telencio**

-BIOGRAPHY-

THE
MARATHON
OF
GREATNESS

NIPSEY HUSSLE

# CONTENTS

# INTRODUCTION

This in-depth biography of Nipsey Hussle, the hip-hop mogul, artist, and activist whose transformative legacy inspired a generation with his inspirational lyrics and visionary business savvy, before he was tragically shot down in the neighbourhood he was committed to uplifting, is described as a "beautiful tribute to a legendary artist" (Quincy Jones).

"The Marathon" was more than just the name of a clothing brand or a mixtape for Nipsey Hussle; it represented his way of life, his unrelenting quest for greatness, and the perseverance needed to face challenges day after day. Hussle was adamant about entering the winner's circle with his entire community because he was determined to win the race to success on his own terms.

The Marathon Don't Stop, a stirring and forceful examination of an outstanding artist, places Hussle in historical perspective and explores his complicated legacy.

# CHAPTER 1

# ON HOOD

If a person's name determines their future, Ermias Joseph Asghedom has been marked for greatness from his birth on August 15, 1985. In Eritrea's Tigrinya language, the name Ermias means "God will rise." His father chose the name, saying subsequently that his son "was sent by God to give some love to bring us together." In February 1992, Ermias was six years old when the teen rap duo Kris Kross released "Jump," which topped the pop charts for eight weeks straight. He was soon Totally Krossed Out, like the rest of America's youth, gaining major inspiration from the pint-sized Atlanta rap sensations born Chris Smith and Chris Kelly, but better known as Daddy Mac and Mac Daddy. "I thought I was gonna be like Kris Kross," Ermias admitted later on the Rap Radar show. He began writing his own raps with a specific goal in mind. "My goal was to be signed and crackin' as a little kid by the time I was twelve or thirteen," he stated. "I was disappointed when I wasn't transformed into Bow Wow."

Ermias rode public transportation as a student at Edwin Markham Middle School, home of the Soaring Eagles. If his mother did not drop him off, he would take the Blue Line of the Los Angeles Metro to and from Watts, where his favourite teacher was Merelean Wilson. Ms. Wilson, who was born in Compton, worked at NASA before dedicating herself to school, and she, like all great teachers, had a knack of bringing out the best in her students.

Ermias used to tell mom, "I'm going to be a rapper," while tapping out a beat with two pencils, but he was serious about his studies. Ms. Wilson recalls him as a straight-A student who ate lunch with her to ensure he understood his homework. Ermias, twelve, wrote a poignant inscription in her 1997 yearbook in unsteady cursive style. "Dear Mrs. M. Wilson, I shall always love you despite the hardships and long days." In her 1999 yearbook, his handwriting was a little looser, and the sentiment was more joyful. "To: Miss Wilson," wrote Ermias, fourteen, "you were my favourite teacher and friend at Markham." Please never stop teaching since everyone in Markham needs a little piece of you. Always with love, Asghedom, Ermias." He wrote "Class of '99' next to his signature. "Whop!! Whop!!" he exclaimed, drawing the year in large bubble letters. Meanwhile, Ermias continued to pursue his own musical passion, aiming for teenage stardom. His mother was unable to pay for studio time, but she did locate a free music lesson for him. She would drop him off at the Watts Towers Arts Center on Saturdays to learn with a classically trained composer. "He taught us how to use the MPC, which is the beat machine, which is a sixteen-track recorder," Nipsey said. "That was my first exposure to production." Ermias could activate an infinite number of drum sounds and samples by tapping on the MPC's four rows of rubber pads. Every beat, however, began with the sound of a metronome counting down the time. Tick-tick-tick. "My moms would always see me writing raps and all that, listening to CDs and buying' The Source magazines,' ' Hussle later explained. "She was just like, 'I know you're really into your music.'" I'll start dropping you off if you want.``

When Ermias learned that Lewis had studio equipment, he immediately invited himself over to work. "Him and Rimpau ended up being regular guests at the house," Lewis remembers of his musical family with deep roots in South Los Angeles. His mother was the principal of Crenshaw's Fifty-Fourth Street Elementary School and wholeheartedly supported her son's musical ambitions. At the time, he was known as EQ, but he would eventually be known as Ralo Stylez. They listened to music for hours on end. Staying up to date on the latest rap releases quickly became more than a hobby for Ermias. He made it a business. Using their computer skills, he, Rimpau, and Ralo would create their own mix CDs and sell them at school for $5 each.Ermias learned at a young age that deserving and gaining respect are not the same thing. He was fifteen when he stopped attending Hamilton High, although he didn't actually drop out, contrary to popular opinion. "I got kicked out and went to boot camp for a little while," he explained in a Complex interview in

2010. "They tried to accuse me of being involved in a school robbery." A computer lab was broken into, and all of the computers were stolen." Despite his well-documented interest in computers, Ermy maintained his innocence, telling Complex, "I didn't do it!" with a giggle. Taking him at his word—because honesty was his philosophy in general—Hussle's first run-in with the law was being blamed for someone else's crime.

Ermias had no choice but to take it on the chin and keep pushing after an emotional hearing. "My mom went to my court date and expressed her frustration," he recounted. "They were all like, 'We got a place for him, don't trip.'" He attended a youth program run by the sheriff's department in Lennox. "It wasn't a penitentiary," he explained. "If you screw up in school, you get kicked out." Ermias, never one to submit to authority, had completed traditional education, but his thirst for knowledge persisted. "I didn't want to be looked at as an idiot, and I didn't want to feel uneducated, because I really stopped going to school at fifteen," he told Complex. I was never naive in terms of sitting in schools and learning about various subjects and genuinely soaking it up." He enrolled in a community college in West Los Angeles, taking studies in psychology, English, and philosophy. Ermias managed to achieve A's and B's despite his attention being divided between hustling and music at this stage.

# CHAPTER 2

# START

Hussle arrived at LAX airport with fresh vigour after celebrating his nineteenth birthday in Eritrea. He'd been hustling full-time and rapping part-time before the trip. He was content to pop the trunk and sell CDs hand to hand because he didn't have an outlet to get his music recognized. He knew how to make money, and he made a lot of it, but his activities were not consistent with a broader goal. Hussle realised it was time to strike out on his own. He decided he needed his own studio while standing in the parking lot. He called his man D-Mac, who was seeking to buy the Lincoln, and asked whether he was still interested.They only had enough to set up a studio between the two of them. Nipsey couldn't afford to hire a studio engineer, so he learned how to use Pro Tools on his own. He needed to conserve energy for the following leg of the Marathon. Hussle considered who else was as serious about music as he was. He contacted J Stone, a teenage MC who'd been recording mixtapes on a karaoke machine since elementary school.

One of the things that kept them going was the knowledge that what they were doing was lawful. Hollywood, like the music industry, had struggled to keep up with what studios perceived as digital infringement. Change was unavoidable due to technological advances, and the film industry was divided on how to respond. Some believed that bootlegging had a promotional benefit in terms of attracting new viewers online and on the streets, but the Motion Picture Association of America disagreed. Under demands to crack down on DVD bootleggers, the Los Angeles Police Department established a special anti piracy team. They even detained one of their own. Sam felt the impression he was being observed. Hussle requested that Dexter keep Sam's DVD burners and blank discs at the house. He'd stop by every now and then to get what they needed. Despite Sam's efforts to maintain a low profile, the police raid on November 17, 2006 was a devastating blow. It wasn't his first encounter with the cops, and they smacked him hard. The brothers lost their home and everything in it. "The police really boxed up all my music equipment," Hustle explained. His Apple laptop with Pro Tools was stolen. His hard drives, which contained music and movies, were destroyed. "They took everything," he claimed, "cars, jewellery, everything." "You can get cars, money, and jewellery back." But you can't get a song back. Or a picture. Niggas is no longer alive. People who died and you caught them on camera—a classic scene." The police seized everything of value, including the security cameras that were installed around the property, Sam's bulletproof BMW 745, money stashed in safes, and gold chains. The cops also discovered a firearm registered in Sam's name. "They threw the gun on me because I was on probation and had prior gun cases," Hustle explained. "So, that was a major setback."

Crenshaw's streets were not waiting for a record contract. On June 10, 2007, one of Hussle's neighbourhood homies, Boss Hoss nicknamed BH, was shot in the back of the head. "I was sixteen years old," remembers BH. "I activated code blue. I got back up. "Man, I messed up!" BH vowed to God that if He gave him another chance to live, he would completely transform his life. Sure enough, he began to bounce back. "I learned how to walk again," he explains. "Once Nipsey learned I was okay, he drove up to my house." He was just stunned, as if to say, 'Bro, what the fuck? "We received word that you had died."

"I was," BH admitted.

"You're only sixteen, nigga!" he exclaimed. "You were on the verge of dying! It's time for you to grow up, bro. You must visit this studio. You have to do this shit."

Nip took BH under his wing from then on. "I'd already told myself that I'm not fucking with these lowlife stupid motherfuckers any longer," he explained. "I nearly lost my life dealing with everyone who is still doing dumb shit." It's just not worth it." They opened up shop inside his mother's house on Sixtieth Street. "I made my first song in this room right here," BH explains. "Me and Nip used to sleep in here on the floor, bro." ro Tools—gone. His hard drives, which contained music and movies, were destroyed. "They took everything," he claimed, "cars, jewellery, everything." "You can get cars, money, and jewellery back." But you can't get a song back. Or a picture. Niggas is no longer alive. People who died and you caught them on camera—a classic scene." The police seized everything of value, including the security cameras that were installed around the property, Sam's bulletproof BMW 745, money stashed in safes, and gold chains. The cops also discovered a firearm registered in Sam's name. "They threw the gun on me because I was on probation and had prior gun cases," Hustle explained. "So, that was a major setback."

Dre wasn't the only one who was paying attention. Jonny Shipes, the creator of Cinematic Music Group, had just gotten a job at Epic Records. Shipes had discovered Sean Kingston, a Jamaican youngster residing in Miami whose song "Beautiful Girls" exploded into a big pop hit. But what Shipes truly wanted to do was release some good rap music. Cinematic, which was only just starting at the time, would go on to become one of New York's best indie hip-hop labels.

"Charlie Walk at Epic had given me a label deal and he was like, 'Go find some stuff,'" remembers Shipes. "At the time, West Coast hip-hop was not doing well. I contacted DJ Felli Fel in Los Angeles and said, "Bro, what the fuck is going on?" "Where's the hot shit?" "'Well, there's this kid Nipsey Hussle, but he's deep in the streets,' Felli said. I'm not sure you're going to want to mess with that. He's the real deal.'" When Shipes Googled Nipsey Hussle, a Myspace page appeared. "There were one or two songs on there," he remembers. "'Bullets Ain't Got No Names,' and maybe he had 'I Don't Give a Fucc' too."

Shipes experienced chills as he listened. "I felt like I was standing on Sixtieth and Crenshaw with him," he recalls. He was smitten by the tracks' rawness, the harsh delivery, and the singsong hooks. With every word he spoke, Nipsey Hussle was painting a picture. "It was the rawest shit I had heard in years." He retaliated against Felli, and twenty-four hours later he and his associate Harlem MC Smoke DZA were on a plane to Los Angeles to meet with Hussle and his squad. Hussle and his management decided to put together a mixtape before the Epic agreement was signed. Bullets Ain't Got No Name Vol. 1 was the title. Steve Lobel had a solid working relationship with Power 106 DJ Felli Fel, who was also a producer and recording artist. He consented to host the recording. "Nipsey had a certain IT factor," Felli added. "He had a lot of music, but to be honest, a lot of it wasn't radio material." For me, it was simply seeing that Nip was different. I was just drawn to his work."

Jamaica was nice—the ganja, the jet skis—but as soon as Nipsey returned home, cops found out. The next day, they were waiting at Slauson and Crenshaw to take him to jail. The Men's Central Jail, one of the world's largest correctional facilities, is one of America's worst jails, with a lengthy history of proven abuses. Hussle had money to bail himself out because he'd recently secured a major label deal, but he couldn't access it because he was on probation and the authorities had placed a hold on his cash. To make matters worse, a fight broke out in the holding tank when he arrived at jail. When the situation became critical, Hussle found himself outnumbered by a gang of Bloods. "You already know the county jail," he subsequently explained. "There ain't no homies in there, Six-Owe." My mindset was that I was anticipating it regardless. We had a few minor brawls, but I didn't get packed out or blasted, so I did well." Hussle survived to tell the tale because of an Inglewood Blood who cared about the young Crip. Hussle was transferred to the secure housing unit (SHU), generally known as solitary confinement, after being processed. The psychological stress of being locked up with no human contact is often reserved for inmates who break the rules. Hussle was placed in the SHU for medical reasons in his case. In Jamaica, he was bitten by a spider, and the injury turned into an abscess on his leg. Inmates in the county jail who have medical difficulties are placed on 24-hour lockdown. Hussle was forced to eat, shower, and leave his cell for only one hour every day. "That was a little difficult for me," he admitted.

Hussle had time to think on some of his decisions while sitting alone in his isolated cubicle. "I felt like I fucked up everything I had worked my whole life for," he explained. "I was sitting in my one-man cell, punching bricks, just out of frustration." Hussle was visited by the gang investigation team one day during his two months in prison. He expected them to ask him about hood happenings, attempting to implicate him or pressuring him to reveal information about his homies. He was astonished to see his Myspace page come up on the jail computer when he was escorted into the gang unit's office. "They had my YouTube playing',' he recalls, smiling. "They were also singing the songs by heart." When the gang unit enjoys your music, you know you're popular on the streets. Hussle was torn between laughing in their faces and signing autographs.

During his time on the run, he learned that Tanisha was expecting a baby girl. While incarcerated, he decided to give her the name Emani Dior. "Her name means 'beautiful faith' in Swahili," he says. "I chose Emani for a few reasons." He'd recently gotten a record deal. He was in jail and had no idea when he would be released. He was expecting a child and was not on good terms with the baby's mother at the time. "It was a lot on my mind," he admitted. "And I believe that faith represented where I was at the time." And that was lovely because I ended up getting out of that circumstance and moving on. Aside from that, I just liked how it sounded. My name also begins with an E." When Shipes informed them that the paperwork was complete, Hustle and Robin Hood rushed to New York to sign the contract. They took a flight to Jamaica when the transaction was completed. Sean Kingston was filming a special for MTV's My Super Sweet 16 there, and it seemed like the ideal spot to celebrate, especially because Hussle might face jail time when he returned to Los Angeles.

# CHAPTER 3

# ALL MONEY IN

Hussle didn't have much time for romance at that point in his career. Snoop had publicly supported the young rapper and promised him a position on one of his albums. Nipsey Hussle was described by The Game as "the next biggest thing in L.A., I swear before God." The Compton rapper then backed up his claim by inviting Nipsey to join him on his countrywide LAX tour. Hussle returned to Los Angeles in the summer of 2009 and struck the ground running. His campaign was gaining traction, generating a magnetic energy that drew in new adherents on a daily basis. "L.A. was turning back over," Dom Kennedy, a frequent collaborator with Hussle, adds. "It was a pivotal time, and he was one of the first people to really kick it off."

As the LAX tour came to a close, Nipsey received a Twitter shout-out from Drake, who had just released So Far Gone, one of the most successful mixtapes in rap history. "Nipsey Hu$$le is the hardest out!" Drizzy twitter, and the two were soon planning a collaboration. Their song "Killer" was recorded for Drake's debut album, Thank Me Later, but they chose to let it leak online during the heyday of blog rap. When Drake's tour stopped in Los Angeles, he asked Hussle out to perform "Killer" at the Nokia Theater. Hussle prowled the stage in red Crenshaw regalia, swinging his iced-out Malcolm X chain, while Drake informed the audience, "Tell your favourite rapper... my nigga Nipsey is a killer!"

Nipsey Hussle was in a bad mood when he received a phone call from Steve Lobel one February morning in 2010. "Nip, pull up!" exclaimed his manager, who would occasionally take him on unexpected experiences such as BMX riding at the Fantasy Factory, a funhouse owned by professional skateboarder Rob Dyrdek.

"I'm sick, man," answered Hussle. "I'm already in bed."

"Nah," Maniac Lobel said. "Rise right now. "Raise your hands!"

"Must be serious," Hussle thought to himself as he walked to the place Lobel indicated. "It was all bigwigs there," he subsequently recalled. "I saw Babyface and Celine Dion." Everyone was there, man. It was over if they ever bombed there." Just when he was wondering, "What the fuck am I doing here?" He recognized a familiar face: Snoop.

"Cuz!" "Nip ain't supposed to be here," Hussle stated as he approached the big homie, whose managers instantly responded, "Nip ain't supposed to be here."

"Well, shit," Snoop said. "Me, neither!" When they argued that Snoop was supposed to be there, he retorted, "Well fuck it—we're both supposed to be here!" Hussle had just seen his pal QDIII, the producer of a track for Nipsey's forthcoming independent record. His father, the great Quincy Jones, was introduced to him by QDIII. The man who made "We Are the World" for Africa in 1985 was now doing another for Haiti twenty-five years later. And for some reason, he insisted on having Hussle on the record—and in the video.

"Go get into it!" Q pointed to the studio and told Hussle.

"I'm cool," Hussle replied. "I'm just coming to show my respect."

Q was adamant. "Nah, go 'head!"

Hussle continued to refuse, claiming he didn't know the song's lyrics, but Quincy can be quite convincing. Before Hussle knew it, he was surrounded by hip-hop legends, including LL Cool J, Busta Rhymes,

Kanye West, and Snoop Dogg. Despite his best efforts to blend among the crowd, Hussle was unmistakable in his grey sweatshirt and iced-out Malcolm X chain. He got caught up in the moment and flashed the 60s hand sign. That weekend, Saturday Night Live parodied the song, mocking "half-famous randos like Bizzy Bone and Nipsey Hussle."

Hussle wasn't even irritated when SNL made their joke. He'd spent a lot of time thinking about his brand since leaving Epic, and he was certain that it didn't depend on being as renowned as possible. "Nipsey Hussle can't be Nipsey Hussle if he doesn't celebrate his successes but also his strategy," Jorge Peniche stated. "I believe that's what people gravitate toward. Nipsey Hussle is a natural motivator." Hussle would work like an independent artist even when he was still signed to Epic. "I'm on overdrive, my nigga," he explained. "A lot of musicians receive the deal and settle in. You get the impression that's why they came, but I didn't come for the transaction, homie. I came to meet the folks." As he moved into a new chapter of his career, everything he did, from his songs to his interviews, spoke about empowerment and redemption, chronicling his path as a young independent musician determined to make it no matter how long it took. "Really, all I want to do is say what I have to say and talk to my people." And give 'em some games, entertain 'em, and tell 'em my story. I was able to get a lot off my chest. I've gone through a lot. A lot of my homeboys don't have a voice. This tale needed to be told. The Marathon is the narrative of that.

Hussle had not released new music since The Marathon in late December, a planned hiatus. "The new music has a different sound," remarked Hussle. "I kinda wanted to shock people with it as opposed to drop leaks and warm 'em up to it." The response to The Marathon suggested that he was cultivating a fervent, highly involved fan group. "Now kids tell me I'm the reason they finished school," he rapped on TMC's new song "Road to Riches." "And if it hadn't been for The Marathon, they wouldn't have made it." Hussle felt obligated to uphold that standard, no matter how long it took. He was still obsessively recording new material for TMC just days before the

November 1 release date. "We're almost done," he declared. "We're getting there." We practically got what we needed. But I'm the type of artist who likes to record right up until the last second... My staff can be irritated because we have tight deadlines and such. But it appears that you receive some of your best material during tight times."

Hussle celebrated the release of TMC with a live performance at the House of Blues on Sunset Boulevard on November 4, supported by the band 1500 or Nothin'.66 Hussle had known Larrance Dopson of 1500 since Robin Hood introduced them, and the production collective had a significant influence on TMC's sound.

# CHAPTER 4

# FDT

Nipsey Hussle swayed to the dizzy beat of "All Get Right," track 5 off his Crenshaw mixtape, while bouncing on the balls of his feet like a centre shortly before tip-off. Tonight was the fulfilment of a promise, a secret event to thank the superfans who "kept it one hundred" and supported Hussle's game-changing Proud2Pay project by purchasing physical copies of Crenshaw for $100 each—turning common thinking about the status of the music industry on its head. "Nipsey changed the game," said renowned rap DJ and broadcaster Sway Calloway, who proudly handed over $100 cash to Hussle live on the air. " 'I know y'all give stuff away for free, but not me!' I'm not interested in $11.99! I don't want to pay $15.99! "I want $100 for my efforts!" That night, there was no velvet rope, no stage; Hussle was standing on his fans' level.

On the final day of Black History Month, February 29, 2016, Donald Trump held a campaign rally at Valdosta State University, which is located in southern Georgia near the Florida state boundary. Despite the fact that the student body is currently over 34% Black, the school's website states that "prior to 1963, the African American presence at Valdosta State was limited to staff in cleaning, cooking, and maintenance positions."

The song was titled "FDT" and was released on March 30, 2016. The internet was enraged by hip-hop's forceful condemnation of the presumed Republican candidate. The final version of the song contained a soundbite of Trump talking about building his "great wall" on the Mexican border (and getting Mexico to pay for it!) as well as footage of Tahjila Davis talking about being kicked out of a Trump rally. "We tryna touch the people," YG said after the song's debut to Billboard. "We're trying to get all of the young people to vote." Take your time because it's vital, you understand? If not, it might be disastrous for us."60 Always utilising music to inspire, Hussle imbued each song with a sense of purpose. The stakes for "FDT" could not have been higher. It was one thing for Snoop to mock Trump after the election, but YG and Nipsey hammered the candidate with a lyrical barrage when it mattered most, encouraging their fans to vote.

# CHAPTER 5

# VICTORY LAP

Hussle's phone was ringing off the hook after Crenshaw's breakthrough. Around that time, he met with 300 Entertainment, a new record label headed by seasoned music executives Lyor Cohen and Todd Moscowitz.

"What's wrong with the record industry is that there are good records," Cohen explained. "It's simple to spot a bad record." It's simple to describe a terrific record. You recognize them immediately away. However, the good records are perplexing." The "good records" were the ones that clogged the pipeline, impeding greatness. That principle was adopted by Hussle in his first rough draft of Victory Lap. "I had a twenty-two-song playlist at first," Hustle explained. With Cohen's counsel in mind, he felt he only had nine truly brilliant songs. So he pared down the playlist and continued to record in the hopes of making more outstanding tracks. "That's the next move," Hussle asserted emphatically during a 2013 appearance on the Sway in the Morning show. "It'll be Victory Lap." The first track is called 'Rap Niggas,' and it will be released at the end of next year."

Hussle was correct about one thing: "Rap Niggas" would be Victory Lap's debut song. There was no doubt in his mind about that. However, it would not be at the top of the list next year—or the year after that. "Rap Niggas" didn't even come out until December 1, 2017. What happened during those four years is a narrative of determination, tragedy, and the triumph of willpower and inventiveness against seemingly impossible difficulties. In other words, the life biography of Nipsey Hussle.

"Nip always wanted 'Rap Niggas' to be his first single," says Rance of 1500 or Nothin', who worked on the music for four years. "This is how I'm going to disrupt the entire music industry," Hussle would remark. "And tell everyone what time it is. And then I'm going to catch their attention and draw them into the true truth that everyone needs to know."

"It ain't even a traditional single," Hussle confessed. "It's not for radio, but it must be said." It makes sense in context. It's everything that's happening. It's everything I stand for right now." What Hussle needed, more than a big song on the radio or celebrity, was to simply proclaim, "I ain't nothin' like you fuckin' rap niggas."

"Rap Niggas" delves into the "gangsta rap" conundrum. As Black Sheep once said, "you can get with this, or you can get with that." Are you a gangster or a rapper? Is it even possible to be both at the same time? And why do people who are one strive to be the other?

The phrase "gangsta rap" was coined by the media to stigmatise rap as an art form when it still appeared viable, before hip-hop became the world's dominant mode of mainstream culture. "Gangsta rap" is a convenient crutch for reporters who specialise in oversimplifying difficult situations and verbatim repeating police talking points. It is mostly employed by those who don't actually listen to hip-hop. Critics of "gangsta rap"—whatever that term actually means—avoid all nuances.

When Hussle said, "I ain't nothin' like you fuckin' rap niggas," he was implying that he was "about that life" in a way that most rappers could never be. "Did the niggas laugh at you in the beginning?" Snoop once asked Hussle about the specific hurdles that artists who grew up in gang culture confront. Informing your crew that you're preparing to become a rapper might be a tricky affair. "I didn't even tell people at first," Hussle admitted. "I wouldn't even tell people I rapped until I had good music that I believed in." Rapping, I felt, was like being an outcast in the streets. Calling yourself a rapper is akin to announcing your retirement. Like you're not with this anymore."

"Like you did with the hood," Snoop observed, smiling. "You've discovered other activities that are a little more relaxing, such as golfing and rapping."

"Exactly!" Hussle responded. "You know, I had to turn it up a notch or two to show that I'm not on any rap shit."5 But, as Tupac once wondered, "Is Frank Sinatra a gangsta singer?" He knew a lot of mobsters, but he never sang about Sam Giancana. Similarly, hip-hop is full of studio gangsters who "wouldn't bust a grape in a fruit fight," as Jay-Z famously stated in "99 Problems." Even before his Marathon series, Hussle's early raps delivered an intelligent critique of gangster life, discussing problems and solutions from a firsthand perspective to help generate healthy dialogue. "I've got a lot of concepts and titles that revolve around the state of this violent world we live in," Hustle explained during the Bullets Ain't Got No Name era. "I have this viewpoint one second, but on the next record, I might take a different viewpoint and speak on this topic from the perspective of intelligence, of someone who wants to change this problem, of someone who wants to resolve the conflict."

"Hussle in the House" and other songs are written from the perspective of "someone who is actively involved." "Hussla Hoodsta" is a song about someone who feels trapped. "Granny, they're still shooting',' ' he rapped. "I can't get no sleep / And it's too late to change 'cause I'm in too deep."

Rather than inciting controversy for the purpose of controversy or getting caught up in media arguments about music and morality, Hussle attempted to portray a wider picture to people caught up in the gang lifestyle as well as those who would unfairly criticise them. "A lot of my homeboys, including myself, felt like there were no options left at one point," he explained. "Like, there weren't any other decisions to be made than the ones we made in terms of gangbanging, being in the streets, bringing violence to other niggas with the same skin color as you, coming from similar struggles as you."

The remedy, as the name of Big U's gang-prevention group suggested, was to develop options. "Give a nigga another option," stated Hussle. "Like opening up the studio and allowing niggas access, or lowering camera prices and making them available to niggas like us." They're going to fall back and do that 90% of the time." When Hussle drew a line in the sand to differentiate himself from "Rap Niggas," he wasn't doing so because he was more "gangsta" than another artist. He was expressing his purpose. Decades of dramatic media coverage of "gangsta rap," including some outright lies, have spread misunderstanding. "The number-one misconception is that everybody in a gang is a mindless killer," Hussle explained, "just an ignorant, self-hating nigga with an Uzi running around killing motherfuckers all day." I'm not going to sit here and defend what's bad. Killing and gangbanging are both wrong. At the same time, the way adolescent kids are treated in these courts is based on, 'Oh, he's a gang member,' so he is treated like a terrorist."

Hussle's most critical message was that the present generation of Los Angeles gang culture is the result, not the cause. "We didn't wake up and decide to create our own mind state and environment," Hustle explained. "Our survival instincts evolved. We don't want our mothers in black standing over our coffins. And being a burden on our parents, calling collect and getting upset because the motherfuckers aren't writing or visiting us, and all that. That is not the lifestyle that anyone wishes for themselves, but it is the result of the lifestyle we live." The true purpose for Hussle was redemption.

Most rap fans associate the title Victory Lap with Nipsey Hussle sitting back in his Maybach with the ceiling missing and one finger in the air, as if directing a symphony from behind the wheel of his European whip. The classic cover art has become so associated with the Grammy-nominated album that Jorge Peniche revealed his initial Victory Lap CD booklet concepts on Instagram. The designs, which incorporate Hussle's handwritten lyrics to a song that has yet to be released, tell volumes. "You could," he said. "I could do it as well." I worked hard till I got it. Nigga, you should as well."

The Marathon was never intended to be a spectator sport. Nipsey considered all of his true admirers as people running their own races, as reflected by the name of his website, iHussle. Win Lap was always intended to be a joint win for Hussle and his fans.

The idea appeals to Dr. Melina Abdullah of Black Lives Matter, who met Hussle and spoke with him about cooperative economics. She believes that some of that sense of shared fate has been lost in the decades since his death. "That's something that bothers me about the aftermath of his death," she explains. "They're trying to elevate him as this super-capitalist, which is not at all consistent with what I know his intent was." There's nothing wrong with owning good things—Rolexes, Cuban links, and luxury automobiles are all wonderful. However, Hussle's aim extended far beyond amassing fortune for himself and his family. According to Dr. Abdullah, "it was about empowering an entire community."

Hussle stated that he first mentioned Victory Lap in 2012, therefore the title's meaning may have developed over time. "I just know that I wanted my debut album, the one we went to retail with, to be called Victory Lap," Hussle told me days after the record's release. The victory lap, sometimes known as the "lap of honour," is a motorsports custom in which the winning driver drives one more round around the track, usually at a slower speed, saluting the fans and soaking in their affection. It was intended to be a communal experience.

There were numerous wins to be celebrated, beginning with simply being alive, handling business, and becoming an independent success. "Coming' off the major label," Hustle explained, "having' to rebuild the brand on my own, taking' risks, spendin' my own money, doin' things unconventional—like you said earlier, the hundred-dollar album and just being' somewhat of a radical, and it working' in my favour."

Six years after Hussle coined the moniker, Victory Lap still checked all of the conditions. "But a lot has changed since I first started promoting it," he explained. "It's clear that Nipsey Hussle has a clear lane in the game—and he built it and took the stairs to get there." We had options to be aided, but we chose to do it ourselves." Initially, Hussle regarded Victory Lap as the conclusion of the Marathon mixtape series, which proven to be a motivator for a large portion of his fan base. "I wanted the album release to represent the end of the completely independent, do-it-on-our-own mode and the beginning of a new partnership," he explained. The victory for the All Money In label would mean "establishing a new partnership that was in our favour this time," Hustle explained. "And more in the direction of what we came in trying to establish."

Hussle first met Craig Kallman, the chairman and CEO of Atlantic Records, in 2012, before Crenshaw was released. He admired Kallman for being a former DJ who founded his own independent label, Big Beat Records, and let Biggie Smalls to become a label head in his own right, releasing artists such as Lil' Kim and Junior M.A.F.I.A. "We had been talking for a while once I got out of the Epic situation," Hustle explained. "I began doing Marathon mixtapes and touring." I intended to enter the building using certain terms... They didn't think I could justify my demands at the time, which was probably true. So I continued to work."

After negotiating with a few major companies, Hussle began pushing Victory Lap as a mixtape. He thought he was close to a deal, which he intended to announce after Victory Lap and then transition into album mode. But Hussle soon realised that record labels were unwilling to allow him any kind of creative control. "They want to give you a check," he explained. "I told them to keep the check, give me an asset, and let me just market and distribute my shit." He preferred to be involved as a partner rather than receive a large advance. "Niggas couldn't do that," he said. "And it's not because the label didn't want to help me." It's because their companies' corporate structures prohibit ownership. And that offends me."

Hussle abruptly altered his intentions. "I called an audible," he explained. "I knew in my heart that if I didn't stand up for what I believed in, I'd be less of a man." It struck me as racist. As if I don't deserve something I made myself? Do you want to offer me money? Oh, you don't believe I know what the asset is? "Do you think I don't know where the real value is?" His objective had shifted, as had his concept of triumph. "I didn't issue a press release or tell anyone about it," he explained. "I just let my demonstration speak." He stated that his Proud2Pay approach with Crenshaw was just the start. "That's only a small part of my plan."

Following the Crenshaw breakthrough, Hustle and Kallman discussed a possible relationship at Atlantic. "We sat back down at the table and figured out what the deal structure would be," he explained. "And then I did a couple more mixtapes before we actually inked the deal."

All Money In discreetly negotiated a deal with Atlantic in 2015, keeping the details under wraps. "It wasn't the illusion of independence," Hussle revealed to Charlamagne on The Breakfast Club years later. "I understood that no one cares about the agreement. That is a commercial matter. Music is important to people."

Hussle chose to postpone the reveal until fresh music was available. "Nobody knew that," Ralo explained. "But, when you're with a label, it's going to be in your best interest—not only in your best interest, but probably required—that you work with the producers who are already in bed with the company." As a result, while work on Hussle's major label debut began, Ralo found himself on the outside looking in. "Me and Nip, we weren't talking," remembers Ralo. But when he saw the Victory Lap track credits, he knew he had to contact them. "I texted him and told him, 'Thank you,'" Ralo explains. "I was surprised, and two songs from the project that I co-produced."

Although he was capable of producing and engineering his own sessions, Hussle had established a musical team, the centre of which was 1500 or Nothin', the production/composing duo helmed by Larrance Dopson. Dopson, better known to Nip as "Real Rance Fresh," was Hussle's "day-one A-one," putting together a band with some of his church musician buddies, including James Fauntleroy, Lamar "My Guy Mars" Edwards, Charles "Uncle Chucc" Hamilton, and Brody Brown. Working with 1500 taught Hussle that he could rock out with live musicians while still sounding like a rapper. "I've been up there where you get a band and, you know, it turns into the Playboy Jazz Festival," he jokingly said. "There's nothing wrong with that; it's just that the songs sound different."

1500 introduced Hussle to Mike & Keys, formerly known as the Futuristiks, the producing duo. They first collaborated with Hussle on Crenshaw songs such as "Checc Me Out" and "Blessings." Mike and Keys had become "the home team" since then, and all they needed now was their own playground. Hussle put a large portion of the money from his Crenshaw tour into a new studio he dubbed "the compound." It wasn't cheap to build up his own studio, but Hussle has always prioritised ownership. "When you make money," he says, "I believe in investing in yourself." "You could easily go to a lot of places, but I just feel like your foundation should be strong."

They selected a place in Burbank and renovated it for a year and a half. "It was like an open space," he described it. "We built the walls and the acoustics from the ground up." The modifications required a significant amount of time and effort, as well as a six-figure investment. There were four rooms in the compound, two for producers and two for artists and composers, as well as two office spaces. "I had the logos up on the wall," Hustle explained. "I had all of my meetings there." I had an entire video editing room to myself. I had a strategy for finishing this album." As All Money In developed into digital video and cinema, the site contained capabilities for shooting material and postproduction.

For Hussle, the studio was the realisation of a dream he'd had for most of his life. He arranged his bookshelves and whiteboards with short- and long-term goals. He couldn't wait to get started. "Nip used to pick me up at seven o'clock in the morning every single day," Money Mike of Mike & Keys remembers. "Everything he did, he was three or four steps ahead of niggas in terms of what he was trying to do." Even we are creating. He made certain we were always together. Nobody ever brings it up, you know, us being Black men. Working together and being in the same area is difficult."

"It's critical to really tap in," France added in the 1500's. "Any artist with whom we collaborate, we live in that artist." And it's basically just a background score to life.``

In addition to Mike & Keys and the 1500 or Nothin' crew, Hussle enlisted the help of prominent producers such as Bink! and L.A. icon DJ Battlecat to boost the creative chemistry surrounding Victory Lap. New songs were being written, and old songs were being reinvented, enlarged, and given new life.

"Real Big," or "Rescue Me," according to the original session file name, was one of the first tracks Hussle recorded for Victory Lap. "We had done it at 1500 studio in Inglewood and then brought it to my new studio in Burbank to just add layers to it," Hustle explained. "That's one of my favourite records off Victory Lap."

1500 and Bink! decided to bring in some extras to give the record additional substance. "I stepped outside for a minute," Hustle explained. "When I returned, Bink! was there. Battlecat was present. Marsha from Floetry was present. It was as though I had strolled into a room full of magnificence. And everyone was on a keyboard, Marsha was singing in the booth, and Bink! was on the console. The Roger and Zapp machine was being played by Battlecat. And it seemed as if the record was coming to life. Walking in and seeing everyone working on my record was awesome. That was something that really motivated me."

"That was probably the most special song I feel like we did with Nip," Money Mike explained. "When Rance made Nip record this song, we never would've guessed Nipsey would record on a beat like that." There's no snare, no nothing but a kick and a high hat."

"That's literally a storytellin' song, bro," Rance remarked, calling Hussle "one of the best storytellers alive" a year after his death. "That was one of my favourite songs because he sang the hook." the was my favorite portion because the nigga had a great voice!"

All of the instrumental prowess drove Hussle's lyrics to new heights. "I'm not even going to make a front," he added. "I did go insane while making the Victory Lap." I did. I was only an artist. So I didn't hold back. I didn't hold back and kept my business program, business sleep, business wakeup time, and business daily schedule intact. "I just became a pure artist."

Hussle was confident he was performing his best job ever. "The radical exercise that took place on this project is what I'm most proud of," he remarked. Finally, he was able to dive all the way in and demonstrate his abilities. "You gotta mine for diamonds on the earth, and that's a dangerous job," he explained. "People do die." Hussle viewed the creative process similarly. "To mine for your art, you have to dig for it." Music is like that, but it's risky to go mining for your own worth."

Making music was a spiritual experience for Hussle. "Anyone who messes with music for a long enough time—if you don't cloud yourself and miss it—you'll realise it's spiritual," he remarked. "Vibrations are the word if you're in tune and present enough." As a result, the term has tremendous power. It's true."

Victory Lap was primarily a collection of anecdotes about Hussle's life. "You've put out so much music," Elliott Wilson of the Rap Radar podcast asked Hussle, "how is there still so much that hasn't been expressed?"

Hussle's response seems apparent, but it was deep in its simplicity. "Man, it's just a lot of things that happened," he admitted.

"Every year, there were thousands of murders in Los Angeles." So we did what we did in that context as well. We were not removed. I'm a little removed now since I'm prosperous and have places to go. But I wasn't separated from developing projects and coming to the studio. I was standing right here. So all of that happened. There are a lot of stories."

Hussle's objective was to inspire even as he reviewed his own difficulties and tragedies. "I want a soundtrack for my penthouse," he informed Mike and Keys. I'd like to have a soundtrack for my Maybach. I'd like to have a soundtrack for my workspace. I want to feel the way I do when I get in my car, wake up in my position, and stare out the window... Not a nigga from the streets coming and succeeding, but a long-distance pursuit. And, at the end, celebrating your success. That's how I envision the song sounding."

The online music media cycle's short attention span is eager to throw around terms like "classic" and "timeless," words that take on significance only with the passage of time. But, in order to give his debut album more lasting power, Hussle paid special attention to outstanding music from the past while working on it. Although he had no way of knowing that Victory Lap would be his only record released during his lifetime, he surely gave it his all.

"When you think about the production that's popular right now, and when you make a project that doesn't necessarily sound like right now, I think that lends toward the music being received as being outside of time," he explained. "I study music as well as artists and careers." And when you look at albums that have sold ten million copies—even outside of hip-hop—like Tracy Chapman, Adele's, or even Nelly or Eminem's second album, the production is not fashionable ninety percent of the time. It has a musical foundation. It's based on chords and instruments, as well as music's conventional brilliance".

Hussle and his colleagues headed over to Europe in early 2015.

"I felt at home," Hustle said following an explosive performance at Islington's O2 Academy. "I felt like I was in Los Angeles.... That, to me, is the best part of this. You can obtain media attention and money—obviously, money is the motivating factor. But when you receive genuine affection back from the people. Someone is genuinely yelling your lyrics. That is one of the biggest rewards for your efforts. It's a form of reinforcement. That is the reason we do it."

Hussle was looking forward to getting back to work at his studio on his drive back to LAX. He was eager to check how the Victory Lap sessions were progressing and to put the finishing touches on the remodelling. But he was going to learn some unpleasant news concerning the studio. Hussle had been paying rent to a man he assumed was the building's owner. He was, in reality, subletting the space. When the All Money In team received an eviction notice giving them days to evacuate the premises, they were still finishing up the building. "It was just some political paperwork shit that went bad," Hustle explained.

He attempted to speak with the proprietors, explaining that he had not realised the space was a sublet. He offered to pay the first year's rent in advance. "They just said, 'Nah, we cool.'" "We ain't fucking with you," Hussle recalls. "They ain't really given me no reason." He appeared in court armed with papers, receipts, and bank records. "I never missed a rent payment. Hussle explained, "Everything was always on time." "The judge was like, 'Brother, none of that means shit.'" Police arrived on the third day and expelled them from the complex.

"That set me back," Hustle explained. "We had to rethink our entire strategy." We suffered a significant financial loss. We had also grown accustomed to the workplace environment. It just all fell apart in the middle of the process, so that one stung a lot."

More of a person's character is revealed by how they handle hardship than by how they celebrate victory. Hussle was given numerous options for seeking vengeance. "I'm going to burn down the building," they declared. "Let me fuck this building up." Hussle and his crew had built the walls and the floors. It would have been easy to react violently. "I just told everybody to chill," recalls Hussle. "We're not doing anything." We'll just take that one for the team."

As much as it stung to lose the studio where he'd planned to finish success Lap, Hussle found success in how he handled the setback.

"They robbed me, in essence," Hustle explained. "Something was taken from me. They ended up preserving much of the walls and structure for their next renter." It wouldn't have been difficult for Hussle to respond. He only needed to say yes. Instead, he decided to let the universe balance things out. "It's cool," he stated. "I don't take it as anything other than a higher energy moving me out of that space."

The Victory Lap sessions have returned to the 1500 Sound Academy in Inglewood. In addition, Hussle rented studio space at Paramount Recording Studios. He put himself back into the creative process.

On the 14th of August, 2015, the N.W.Straight Outta Compton was released in theatres around the country and dominated the box office for several weeks. The film, directed by F. Gary Gray and produced by Dr. Dre and Ice Cube, was a massive production with a $28 million budget.43 People have been telling Hussle his entire career how much he resembled Snoop. He was the obvious option to play Snoop on film. "Snoop called me," Hustle explained. "Ted called me—one of his business partners—before Snoop. People have sought out to Ted before Dre. Previously, F. Gary Gray, the filmmaker." "Those dudes are icons and legends," Hussle told them all. And they are the individuals I grew up listening to and idolising. However, I studied branding. And one of the commandments is that you don't walk in the shoes of a great man."

Hussle spent a long time discussing his decision with Snoop since he treasured their connection so highly. "I just had to respectfully say, 'Nah, I can't do it,'" Hussle said. "I think I coulda pulled it off authentically," he added, "because I grew up on Snoop and know his lyrics by heart." "But I just feel like it's people in America and around the world who haven't heard of Nipsey Hussle or been exposed to what I do yet." That could be their first exposure to it as an actor portraying Snoop."

As a result of the discussions around Straight Outta Compton, Hussle eventually got into the studio with Dr. Dre, which had been an ambition of his for years, whether he liked to admit it or not. "I just heard the soundtrack," he explained to Big Boy. "It's going to be epic." And I would have liked to have been involved in a different capacity, because I did music on the soundtrack with Dre." However, Hussle's songs were not included in Dre's third solo album, Compton, which was released one week before the film.

Hussle did, however, appear as himself in the pilot episode of Rachel Bloom's critically praised CW musical comedy series Crazy Ex-

Girlfriend that year. Hussle's legendary cameo made fun of rap-star machismo in a song called "The Sexy Getting Ready Song." While Rachel's character, Rebecca Bunch, is getting ready for a date by squeezing into Spanx and tweezing and waxing her hair, Hussle appears in the bathroom rapping, "Hop on my dick in that tight little dress..." He comes to a quick halt as he spots the mess on her bathroom sink. "God," he exclaims, stunned. "This is how you get ready?" Rebecca gives a nod. "It's terrifying. Something out of a horror film. "Like some nasty-ass patriarchal nonsense." Hussle makes an excuse for himself. "Do you know what?" I have to apologise to certain ladies."

"He was so sweet and funny," Aline Brosh McKenna, the show's co creator, recalls. "He was just game," Bloom recalls of his time working with Hussle. "He brought his girlfriend on set, and I remember her thinking the song was really funny."

The authors were so taken with his performance that they devised a closing part for the show in which he goes through a list of "Bitches to Apologise To" and calls them up one by one. Hussle called in lines like: Hey, Denise? Nipsey Hussle here. Earlier today, I experienced an eye-opening event. I'm phoning to apologise for how I treated you in my latest music video while you danced. Denise, I apologise for showering you with Cristal. I never even asked if you liked champagne. And it most likely ruined your blowout.

Anyway, Denise, please contact me as soon as you receive this. I'd want to talk about Simone de Beauvoir's The Second Sex, which I recently finished. You are stunning on the inside and out. You are on par with me.

Lauren found out she was pregnant with the couple's first child a few months after that program aired. It was exciting news, but it imposed a difficult decision. She'd been chosen for a key role in John Singleton's TV drama Snowfall. "It was her dream role," Hussle remarked. "It was by far the most difficult decision of my career,"

Lauren told GQ. She declined the offer and chose motherhood while supporting Hussle as he pursued his artistic dreams.

Hussle wants Victory Lap to outperform all expectations after devoting so many years to it. He was becoming an obsessive perfectionist in the process. "I listened to Quincy Jones interviews," Hussle said. "I was watching how he mixed Thriller, and how they had ten songs to mix. He returned his attention and asked, 'What are the three weakest links?' They got rid of them. And since they got rid of three of them, they got 'P.Y.T.' and two more monster records that you probably can't believe weren't on the original round of the album."

Quincy wasn't available to consult on Victory Lap, but when Lauren invited Hussle to her friend Cassie's birthday party on August 26, he drew the attention of another superproducer. "I've known Puff for a while, but we had a good conversation at Cassie's birthday party," Hussle recalls. "He was like, 'I'm in Los Angeles, man, come through.'" Let's listen to some music.' So I took the record over there."

Puff was impressed by what he heard. Initially, Hussle was attempting to persuade him to appear in the video for "Rap Niggas." He referred to Puff's role in Nas' video "Hate Me Now" as an example. "I want you to put the mink on, get in the video, and we're gonna make a movie," Hussle stated. Puff explained to him why the video was so popular. "Bro, I busted a forty-million-dollar check the week before I did that video," Puff explained. "I went out and spent all this money on a chain and tigers because I received the biggest check of my life." We're not going to be able to recreate that energy." But upon listening to "Rap Niggas," Puffy had some thoughts. Hussle listened intently.

"Yeah, that shittight, bro," Puff said. "But there's something missing." Hussle was initially dissatisfied because the record had already been mixed and mastered. "I see what you're trying to do with this," Puffy replied, pulling up a record called "Natural Born Killaz" by Ice Cube and Dr. Dre. It sounded ten times louder than Hussle's first single. "This is your standard," Puffy said. "Until your shit knocks like this, it's not doing its job."

Hussle summoned Rance and Mars from 1500 to the studio in order to make it bigger and better. "This is a West Coast anthem," Hustle explained, before playing "Natural Born Killaz" for them as a reference. "They took the record to the next level," Hussle stated proudly. "We believed we were finished with it.

One of the most influential West Coast rap albums of the previous decade was created by a Harlem hitmaker—now living in Los Angeles—who was once at the forefront of rap's bicoastal conflict.

Puff suggested that Hussle delete several tracks off Victory Lap. "Nip, you got a classic album," Hussle recalls. "Many legends don't have classic records, dude. "I'm not just throwing that word around." "I been ridin' to it in the Maybach," Puffy explained. I've been listening to it from start to finish. Take a handful of these songs out and it'll stand on its own." Hustle followed his advice. Puff also enlisted the help of Scott Storch and Mario Winans to play on a few tracks, and sat in on a second round of mixing.

Puffy's most famous contribution was his vocal performance on "Young Niggas," a single based on a sample from PartyNextDoor's "West District." "This is the one, bro!" When he heard the song, Puff exclaimed. "I'm excited about this one." During Puff's vocal takes, Hussle kept the energy in the studio high.

Hussle paid tribute to Lauren in an Instagram post in the summer of 2017: "My muse for the last 4 years... a lot of her energy went into this new album... I'm sure I owe her some publicity. I did, however, give her a baby, so Lady Hussle's contributions to Victory Lap extended beyond her role as muse. The words "victory lap" can be heard between tracks. Hussle's soulmate also appeared in various music videos as an actress. "She's been making my shit go viral," Nip said. London also made it a point to communicate her feelings about the song. "Sometimes she'll be in the studio and she won't say nothin' if she doesn't like it," Hussle recounted. "If she feels something, she'll say something." Among the tracks she approved of were "Rap Niggas" and "Young Niggas." Lauren had to confess she was impressed after listening to the record from beginning to end in his car. "This shit is a clear elevation from what you've been doin'," she said. "I'm not saying your shit wasn't tight, but you're going to wake a lot of people up."

To create such a tremendous body of work over a long period of time, Hussle had to endure the loss of family time and time again. "How much sacrifice did you have to make to get to this point?" on-air personality Hardbody Kiotti of 97.9 FM asked Hussle when the Victory Lap promo run would come to an end. Houston's The Box.

"Man," Hussle responded after a little pause. "Everything."

There were never enough hours in the day for an artist, entrepreneur running numerous firms, and father. "Everything gets tested," Hussle stated matter-of-factly. "Your relationships are put to the test. All of it. It's difficult to explain to the kids."

Hussle previously stated that he used to keep Emani away from the studio. "There were a lot of men in the studio," he explained. "And it was just a certain energy that I don't want to overexpose my daughter to." But, given how much time he was spending on Victory Lap, he reconsidered his policy. "This is my life," he explained. "So I can't separate my children." That cannot be the reason we are unable to spend time together." He reflected on how many Bob Marley interviews he had seen when youngsters were present in the background. "It's gonna be weed lit," he predicted. "It'll be everything you try to keep your children away from." But the kids will be right on deck."

Hussle created a specific space for Emani to hang out in while visiting the studio, and he imposed some basic rules. "We ain't gonna talk like that with my daughter in here," he said. Hussle arranged for someone to keep Emani entertained with cartoons and food while he was at work. "She can kinda peep what I'm doing and get a better understanding," he explained. " 'He ain't just avoiding me. He's truly here working."

Kiotti, a former artist and rapper who moved into radio, said one of his favourite songs on Victory Lap was "Dedication," for obvious and not-so-obvious reasons. "You've gotta love this shit," he exclaimed. "It's a lot that comes with this."

Hussle enthusiastically agreed. "One hundred percent," he stated. "If you don't enjoy it, you'll give up." You're gonna throw in the towel, for sure. And if you're not willing to die and lose everything, you won't make it. And you're not going to die. "Do you understand what I'm saying?"

"You're gonna pass out before you die," Kiotti jokes.

"But you're gonna have to be okay with dying for this shit," Hussle remarked flatly. "It's similar to gangbangin'." You can't be a true banger unless you're willing to die and go through life. You won't be able to function in this environment. Not to suggest that's what you want, but you'll have to accept it as a part of life."

"Dedication," one of the most dramatic tracks on Victory Lap, was one of the first songs produced for the project. Finishing it was a marathon in and of itself—and a team effort. Ralo Stylez created the original beat in 2012. Hussle dropped a hook two weeks after Crenshaw dropped that felt crucial right away. "I knew that this message that I'm expressing or this group of words belongs on an album called Victory Lap," Hustle explained. "I haven't even started writing the verses yet." Within a year or two, he had written a couple verses, but the song felt incomplete. "I know what it is," Hussle remarked, as if he could feel its power. "I'm just not there right now to write it."

Hussle's music team would always inquire about "Dedication" as mixtape after mixtape—Mailbox Money in 2014, Slauson Boy 2 in 2016, No Pressure in 2017—arrived. "You sleepin' on that record, bro,' ' they'd say. "I'm not sleeping on it," Hussle would say. "I'm just waiting for the right amount of energy to finish the song."

"We went through at least six different versions of that song," Rance explained.

"This is one of those songs where he only had one verse for like six years," Money Mike continued. "And I recall saying, 'We gotta get Nip to rap on it, bro.'" Let's just go in there and press him right now."

Hussle was accompanied by Lauren, his mother, and his grandmother to the red carpet premiere of the Tupac Shakur film All Eyez on Me on June 14, 2017. "Mom was always a big Pac fan," he said. "She said she went to see the movie at the Magic Johnson Theatre." "I said, 'Cool, do that, but we're going to the premiere as well.'"

While walking through the parking lot, Hussle ran across Kendrick Lamar, who had a stronger bond with Tupac than other California rappers. As a child, Lamar witnessed Shakur filming a music video in his neighbourhood. Pac has appeared to him in a vision since then, and his most recent album, To Pimp a Butterfly, had an extended dialogue with Tupac's ghost.

The two wordsmiths exchanged greetings.

"What's up, bro?" Hussle stated.

"That verse is comin' back, nigga," Lamar said. "That's a shitfire!"

"All right, bet!" "The 'Keyz 2 the City' album?" Hussle inquired.

"Nah," Lamar replied. 'Dedication.' "

Hussle was perplexed. Damn, I'm not even going to mail that, he thought. But this was not the time or place to inquire.

"All right," he replied. "If that's the one you fucked with and you wrote a verse to it, dope."

The premiere included a slew of West Coast rap royalty. The film, on the other hand, was merely adequate. No actor alive could match Shakur's captivating charm, no matter how much the lead actor resembled him physically. Throughout the evening, Hussle had in-depth discussions with Snoop, Lamar, and his label boss, Top Dawg of TDE.

"Top a Blood," Hussle elaborated. "He's from the Bounty Hunters." He's from the Nickerson Gardens development. Snoop is from Long Beach, and he's a Rollin' 20 Crip. Kendrick, a Compton native. He was raised in a Piru area. I was born in the 1960s. So, Top and Snoop, in their age, politics were so fierce that no matter how powerful they were, there were certain things that were simply prohibited. You couldn't get into those kinds of things. But today, Kendrick and I are from a different period." Hustle and Lamar listened to Snoop and Top talk about Death Row-era street dynamics, as shown in the video they'd just seen, which culminates in Shakur's murder at the hands of Southside Crips. "We saw what happened with Death Row," recalls Hussle. "We saw what happens when gangbangin' spills into music and street politics find their way into positions of power." You have the ideal storm for devastation." After a while, Kendrick and Hussle spoke up, adding to the discussion.

"Our generation, you see me and YG, how we politics," Hustle explained. "You can see how all of us represent our tribes, but we can coexist in the music space."

Another good example was TDE. Their HiiiPower movement, which brought together Jay Rock from Bounty Hunters, Kendrick—a "good kid" from a Piru area—and ScHoolboy Q from Hoovers, was all about unification for a better purpose.

It was a new epoch. And if music can bring people together, maybe it can go even further. "The time might be right," Hussle said, "for us to try to use our influence to evolve how we exist."

Hussle, and evidently Lamar, were very moved by the talk. He returned his guest verse on "Dedication" shortly after the premiere, finishing it with a picture of Tupac's spirit watching over the group's chat at his premiere. Hussle was taken aback when he heard it.

He couldn't have asked for more drive or inspiration to finish the song. "I went back in and did my third verse," Hustle explained. "Even in his verse, it feels like a conversation to me, as if an artist were talking to the artist with whom he's featured on the song." As a result, I reacted somewhat to what was said. So it's just a good song. It was one of the reasons I couldn't finish it for three years."

Nipsey wasn't even upset that "Dedication" slipped to Kendrick behind his back. "That wasn't my plan or anything," Hustle explained. "It was just a bunch of people coming together to make that record happen."

The last "Dedication" session was, by all accounts, a memorable event. "It was probably one of the craziest nights ever," said Money Mike. "The energy in the room that night was so intense that I think everyone needed to go outside and get some fresh air."

"I remember Nip telling us to take a picture that day because everyone was there," My Guy Mars said. "When I returned, that nigga was singing!" 'Wait—that's you singing, nigga?' I thought. Let's get started!' And I believed the niggas would fix it.'Because you know how niggas change their stuff. But for him to maintain it and truly demonstrate his musicianship—many people didn't realise he was a real musician. That nigga knew music, which is why he surrounded himself with musical niggas. So that tune was unquestionably unique."

Hussle could have used the three verses he wrote years ago, but it wouldn't have been this song. "I thrive offa that type of rap that's based on life," he remarked after finishing the record. "I mean no disrespect, but it's not only phonetics and aesthetics. It's actual words that accompany an experience."

Tick-tick-tick.

After all the years of planning and preparation that went into Victory Lap, aiming for the ideal beat, the perfect mix, the ultimate moment of inspiration, there came a point when the sound of the ticking clock drowned out everything else, as happens in every creative endeavour.

The final Victory Lap workouts were a blur for Rance. "It was crunch time at the end of the album, and we all went crazy last week," he explained. According to him, up to six songs, including several that became album highlights, would not make the cut. "We had a bunch of radio songs on there," he reminisces. "And we tapped into the culture, and things came out exactly how they came out—for real for real."

"I had some big records," Hustle explained. "I had a record with Cardi B, and another with Future." Songs featuring such bankable singers were almost guaranteed to receive considerable rotation on radio and make an impression on the pop charts, but Hussle was more concerned with the purity of his Victory Lap vision. "I just wanted it to be a person telling their life story over the course of an album," he explained. That's why he always emphasised that he was signed to his own label, All Money In, and had collaborated with a large company to exploit their resources, relationships, and knowledge. Nobody was going to put pressure on him to abandon his creative vision in search of a club banger.

"Last Time That I Checked," Hussle's collaboration with YG, was one of the final Victory Lap songs to be completed. "I wanted to create something for the West Coast that they felt was specifically for them," Hussle said of the song, which he describes as a "anthem for the streets and my generation."

But, according to Hussle's production team, the anthem nearly didn't happen. "I can honestly say, that was a song that never would've happened if France had not pressed," Money Mike remarked. For nearly two years, the tune sat unfinished, with merely a groovy 808 beat and a hook that alluded to a lyric from Young Jeezy's ATL street classic "Trap or Die."

"That was one of those songs that I believed in," Rance explained. "It's all about timing." It's sometimes just God's timing. And if you don't rush it, it will find you. "It's about power versus force," he remarked, referring to one of Hussle's favourite books.

"Nip needed that extra inspiration," Mars explained. "If we gave him the monstrah shit, he'd have an idea." Rance placed his foot down at the last second, saying, "Fuck that! This has to be on the record. I'm putting pressure on. Let's get started!" Mike & Keys reworked the tune to inspire Hussle, who collaborated with YG just in time to make a classic, bringing a strong message of unity to Victory Lap.

43

"I understand art reflecting life, but we grew up on art instructing life," remarked Hussle of the song. Unlike some of YG and Hussle's previous records, "Last Time That I Checked" was written with the explicit intention of schooling a younger generation, showing them how two young Black men survived the L.A. streets and found a way to turn things around and live a more constructive life. "After a while," Hustle explained, "it felt almost like a responsibility for me to give up the game."

Having the track in place helped Victory Lap achieve a greater purpose, giving the project a sense of completion. But something was still missing. Hussle wants to focus on major musical moments and Marathon milestones in order to fully tell his narrative. He made follow-ups to two landmark songs, "Keys 2 the City" and "Blue Laces," a Crip confessional that Hussle initially hoped to convert into a film.

He contacted Mr. Lee, the famed Houston producer who was responsible for the original "Blue Laces." They had spent two weeks together in a condo in New York, courtesy of Jonny Shipes, when they made the first record, and had kept in touch over the years.

Mr. Lee was overjoyed when Hussle called him in February 2017 and said, "Bro, make me a 'Blue Laces 2.'" Mr. Lee returned the beat two days later. He returned to the original sample, "Hospital Prelude of Love Theme" from the Foxy Brown movie soundtrack. Mr. Lee let more of Willie Hutch's vocal rock this time, accelerating the segment when he said "Aw baby it's been so long..." till it sounded unearthly, like angels speaking in tongues. The captivating instrumental generated a tight atmosphere that got Hussle's emotions flowing, as emotional as a bittersweet memory.

That night, Big Reese, a member of Mike & Keys' production team, was in the lab. Hussle characterised him as a San Diego native who "turned into a real positive dude that came out of the struggle." They'd grown close, and Reese had the kind of chemistry with

Hussle that allowed him to push him creatively. "That's tight, Hussle," Reese replied after hearing the first verse. "Where are you going?" Nip informed him that he was leaving and would return the next day.

"Don't leave," Reese instructed. "Do the second verse right now."

Hussle returned to the booth and probed deeper, letting off another stream-of-consciousness flow about Dr. Sebi, the herbalist and healer who died in a Honduran prison in August 2016. Lauren had introduced Nip to Dr. Sebi's nutritional advice, which he found to be quite beneficial. Hussle became interested in Dr. Sebi's story after reading about a court case in which he faced trial for practising medicine without a licence and reportedly demonstrated that he could cure patients with AIDS using herbs and a dietary plan. Hussle was going to film a documentary on Dr. Sebi's life, and had joked in interviews about threats to his own life because the pharmaceutical business didn't want Sebi's herbal remedies to be broadcast, finding it weird that the tale had not been extensively disseminated. "You know how they play," Hussle stated on the radio. "'Hussle, be careful!' Niggas is tweeting me." Your jet is about to crash.' 'Y'all niggas better ride for me,' I say.

"Blue Laces 2" was the first and only time he spoke publicly about Sebi, claiming that the herbalist's death in jail was punishment for "teaching health." (The doctor's family claims he died of malnutrition while imprisoned in Honduras owing to bad prison circumstances.) The rest of the verse discussed Hussle's love for Rick Ross, his business achievements, and his involvement with the Los Angeles City Council.

Big Reese sensed a particular energy in the air. "Blue Laces 2" was quickly becoming a powerful testament in front of his eyes. "Damn, that's tight, bro," he remarked to Hussle. "The second verse is more difficult than the first..." Nip, finish the song right now. You're in a good mood right now. "Please do not leave."

Then Hussle returned to the booth and delivered a verse unlike the two that came before it. It was a flashback to a tragic real-life experience, depicted in devastating detail, rather than a sequence of vivid sensations. "Sometimes you'll be in a luxury car, a penthouse, a first-class flight, or a bomb-ass hotel somewhere and just remember the complete opposite," Hussle later observed. "Being on the run from the cops or driving your buddy to the hospital bleeding." I was just thinking about the battle and all we went through in order to get here." The final stanza of "Blue Laces 2" recounts a gun duel on a beach and its sad aftermath, with the rapper attempting to get his comrade to the hospital before he bleeds out while also calming his distraught lover and dodging cops.

"It was hard for me to get it out," Hussle admitted. "I was overwhelmed by how true it was and how real it was to him." I was taking a break in the booth." He praised Reese for pushing him when he finished recording the song. "Damn, bro," he exclaimed. "You were used by a higher power today."

Hussle felt his task was done after that record was completed. "I knew at that point in my career that I wasn't going to do anything else until I felt like I had an album with fourteen or sixteen great songs," he explained. "My entire plan was to be ready to move when it blew me away." When I listen to it from beginning to end and I get shivers and hear a person in the music, I know I'm ready to leave. "When I heard it, I was like, 'Yeah, it's outta here.'"

After finishing the record, Hussle had more time to devote to his growing family. Kross "The Boss" was born on August 31, 2016—a Leo like his father, with a two-week birthday. Hussle has always enjoyed being a father, despite his initial fear. "Nobody's prepared for that," he remarked. "No way. You're at a loss for what to do. But you're all going to learn together. Mother number one has the instinct, therefore that will kick in. And what's strange about the kid is that he's not actually trippin'. We're cool with a diaper, a bottle, and affection."

The hardest part was making the decision. "The fatherhood part is easy," he explained. What was difficult was staying dedicated to the grind. "Damn, I've got to make some tough decisions," he admitted. Birthdays and Christmas were unavoidable events. "We'll miss the bag for that," he said. "However, I'm sure I missed a cheerleading practice or a tournament, or a parent-teacher conference—that's all part of the game." He would explain to Emani when he had to miss a cherished family occasion to pursue an opportunity. He addressed her as an adult, and even when she expressed disappointment, he believed she could understand.

He was much more picky after having two children of his own. "I'm a sniper," he explained. "I now have two children, a daughter and a son." If it's not about business or employment, I can devote that time to my children." And he never questioned his sacrifices for his family.

Having Kross was a whole other level of excitement. "He was a little sumo wrestler," Hussle jokingly said of his son. "But he extended out. "I believe he will be tall." Hussle grew to six feet three after a late-teenage growth spurt. Seeing a tiny man about the house sent his head racing, including his thoughts on life in the ghetto.

When people approached Hussle for advice, he took it seriously. "What I tell my young folks in the neighbourhood where I grew up... I address them as if they were my kid. I wouldn't advise my son to join a reputable gang just because it's glamorous. I would give my son advice as though I wanted him to win. You are not even permitted to repeat the present rhetoric. You simply cannot. You have to develop your own sense of time." He would never recommend that someone get put on the hood again. Even though he had made that decision, he couldn't envision Kross fighting in the back of the buildings while wearing a blue rag.

The same instruction he would provide to his own son was worth sharing with the rest of the globe. "It's about money, it's economic," he explained. "Without money, your opinions are powerless." So my advice to my young folks is to "start." Participate in music. Make a video with your camera. Even if your father wasn't a rap star, artistic disciplines were nonetheless meritocracies at the entry level. "You can buy your laptop for a thousand dollars and attack it and start something," he explained. "I believe that simply financializing the ideas is the quickest way."

Hussle, Sam, and their father returned to Eritrea in April of 2018. His experience this time was quite different from his first journey home fourteen years before. Hussle recalled, "They had a minivan waiting for me, and I drove into the country." His passport and paperwork were handled in a VIP manner, and his family was accommodated at a hotel. "It was dope just breathing' the air,' ' Hussle stated. Instead of three months, they spent just over a week in Asmara, the capital city. Hussle was short on time. He'd start preparing for the Victory Lap tour as soon as he came home. He made time to meet with Eritrean President Isaias Afwerki, and he also saw his grandmother and cousins, sharing several excellent meals with them. He stood on the cliffs of Asmara, looking down on his father's native hamlet of Adi Kefelet, reflecting on all the changes he'd witnessed.

"Seeing the way the city and everything else has changed is gratifying," Hussle remarked in an interview with TesfaNews, Ethiopia's state news agency. "I'm delighted to be here. The people, food, culture, and way of life are all excellent."

Hussle had made it big as a rapper in the United States, just as he had anticipated when visiting the local record shop on his first trip home. His achievement had earned him many fans in Eritrea. TesfaNews reporter Billion Temesghen had several questions concerning hip-hop and gangs in Los Angeles, and Hussle answered them all in great detail.

"What would hip-hop be in your own words?" Billion Temesghen inquired.

The solution appeared to be so simple that another artist may disregard it or respond with a half-hearted cliché. But not Nipsey Hussle. "It's a vocabulary, an art form, and a culture that was once limited to young people in America but has now spread globally," he explained. "The neighbourhoods where hip-hop emerged had unique environments and situations that drove people to seek a genuine and efficient form of expression." From police brutality to gang cultures, riots, racial discrimination, and other one-of-a-kind occurrences, hip-hop in terms of music and hip-hop in terms of culture and identity grew. The hip-hop community in every corner of America discussed events that occurred across the country. Graffiti and breakdancing were popular in New York, for example. So hip-hop was the equivalent of CNN for what was going on in the streets. Each region had a different strategy, but it was all about the fight for equality and respect for African-Americans.``

When comparing hip-hop and jazz, Hussle stated that music in America was a representation of our difficulties as black people in America. He felt connected to this piece of African-American history even as an Eritrean-American.

"My father is from Eritrea, and because of him, we have always been in touch with our Eritrean ancestry and culture," Hustle explained. "However, we grew up in South Central LA our entire lives." As a result, we were exposed to the culture of Los Angeles, which was gang culture. I was born in 1985 and spent my childhood throughout the 1990s. The Los Angeles riots occurred in 1993. Rodney King, LAPD brutality, and all of the societal concerns that occurred at the time occurred in our neighbourhood."

"Are gangs scary?" Temesghen inquired. "Terrorising?"

"If you grow up in an area where gang activity is prevalent, that becomes a part of who you are," Hussle responded. "I suppose the equivalent metaphor would be coming from a war zone." If you do, you are aware of conflict even as a youngster, and you eventually become a part of it without even realising it. Following that, these people from combat zones become involved in many ways. Some of them become combatants, while others become writers, singers, or politicians. Everyone, in some manner, builds a subliminal link to what he or she was like as a child. And the gang culture is comparable. It may have begun as self-defence, but as it became the dominant culture of South Central Los Angeles, everyone became a part of it... People who are unfamiliar with the terms scary' or 'terrorising' should avoid using them. However, for those who progress in it, it is just a serious matter. It has been present for generations and is hazardous. White gangs were targeting black people. It arose as a form of defence for your own Black people.``

Since the allusion to Nipsey Russell did not resonate in East Africa in 2018, Hussle's Eritrean admirers coined their own moniker for him: "Nebsi." The word in Tigrinya translates to "self," which is also slang for "homeboy" or "homie." Temesghen noted that his Eritrean name meant "self-hustle" or "the hustle of a homie." She inquired whether he wanted to make any corrections for Eritrea's national newspaper.

"Absolutely not," Hussle replied. "I recently learned about the Tigrinya connection to my name, and I'm so glad it makes sense in Tigrinya." There is no reason to correct it. Allow things to be as it is. That's how I intend to keep it with my Eritrean fans and friends."

"Ermias," Temesghen inquired, "is there anything else you want to add before we finish our interview?"

"There is, in fact. I'd like to express how gratifying it is for us to be able to return home and have a country we can call our own, where the leaders, police, politicians, business owners, and entrepreneurs look like us and are in charge of their own destiny, with each having a say in the overall power structure. It's simply stunning. That is not something we are used to in America. We have a stigma about being inferior."

"It is so sad that they make sure that young African-Americans grow up with that ideology," Temesghen remarked.

"Yes, that is sadly the reality," Hussle responded. "However, things are different in Eritrea. If this had been the case in America, there would have been less violence, insanity, drug users, and violent families. You may have a financial advantage in America, but life is not all about money. In Eritrea, there is a strong sense of family, harmony, and respect. You may believe that money is vital, but it is the closeness of families that makes life better. In America, all we can think about is a physical reality in Eritrea. Being a part of it gives me a great deal of pride."

Now that Victory Lap was complete, Hussle began to reflect on those who had helped empower him along the journey. Jonny Shipes was one of the people he contacted. "From 2013 to 2016, we didn't really speak," Shipes explains. "There was no bad blood; we just parted ways." I'd comment on his Instagram, and he'd respond to mine. But we weren't the same as we used to be. We were connected for those five or six years, conversing every day, sleeping in each other's nurseries, doing whatever we had to do to get through."

Then, in 2016, Hustle hit him at random. "Yo man, you did everything you said you were going to do," he said to Shipes. "It's so inspiring to see what you've accomplished, and I never got the chance to thank you." Shipes has worked with a variety of people in the music industry and did not anticipate spontaneous displays of gratitude. It felt great. They caught up and made plans to meet again. "Yo, next time you're in Cali, hit me," Hussle added. "I'll come out, scoop you." Hussle saw Shipes at LAX a few months later, picked him up in the Maybach, and drove him to the studio to listen to Victory Lap. "I've got to make sure I don't get choked up right here," Shipes adds as the memories come flooding back. "The last two years were identical to the first five." "Yo, come by the crib, come by the studio... " It was completely regular. Come by for Lauren's birthday. We're going to have a great time. That was probably simply his method of assuring me and him that everything was well.``

Hussle was great, deal or no deal. Because he held the rights to all of his mixtapes, he was making slightly under $1 million every quarter from streaming and downloads by the end of 2016. Before Victory Lap was even released, he uploaded his Tunecore royalty statement on Instagram, which totaled $908,312. "No flex," the caption said. "Only for motivational purposes." Controlling your catalogue is where the money is."

Nipsey Hussle chose to formalise this portion of his career in October 2016, announcing the creation of the Marathon Agency after years of making wise moves behind the scenes and pioneering unique methods to the entertainment industry. Hussle's godbrother Adam Andebrhan and longstanding Marathon partner Jorge Peniche were among the team's main members, as were two recognizable faces from Hussle's close circle—marketing and branding guru Karen Civil and rap industry A&R Steve Carless, who collaborated closely with Hussle on Victory Lap. Civil and Carless have known each other for a long time, having gone to the same high school in Elizabeth, New Jersey, and collaborating on YG and Jeezy ads. Hussle identified the Marathon Agency as "the new home for the RADICALS... in a social media post." THE REVOLUTIONARIES AND GAME-CHANGERS who believe they can do things their way."

"Absolutely not," Hussle replied. "I recently learned about the Tigrinya connection to my name, and I'm so glad it makes sense in Tigrinya." There is no reason to correct it. Allow things to be as it is. That's how I intend to keep it with my Eritrean fans and friends."

"Ermias," Temesghen inquired, "is there anything else you want to add before we finish our interview?"

"There is, in fact. I'd like to express how gratifying it is for us to be able to return home and have a country we can call our own, where the leaders, police, politicians, business owners, and entrepreneurs look like us and are in charge of their own destiny, with each having a say in the overall power structure. It's simply stunning. That is not something we are used to in America. We have a stigma about being inferior."

"It is so sad that they make sure that young African-Americans grow up with that ideology," Temesghen remarked.

"Yes, that is sadly the reality," Hussle responded. "However, things are different in Eritrea. If this had been the case in America, there would have been less violence, insanity, drug users, and violent families. You may have a financial advantage in America, but life is not all about money. In Eritrea, there is a strong sense of family, harmony, and respect. You may believe that money is vital, but it is the closeness of families that makes life better. In America, all we can think about is a physical reality in Eritrea. Being a part of it gives me a great deal of pride."

Now that Victory Lap was complete, Hussle began to reflect on those who had helped empower him along the journey. Jonny Shipes was one of the people he contacted. "From 2013 to 2016, we didn't really speak," Shipes explains. "There was no bad blood; we just parted ways." I'd comment on his Instagram, and he'd respond to mine. But we weren't the same as we used to be. We were connected for those five or six years, conversing every day, sleeping in each other's nurseries, doing whatever we had to do to get through."

Then, in 2016, Hustle hit him at random. "Yo man, you did everything you said you were going to do," he said to Shipes. "It's so inspiring to see what you've accomplished, and I never got the chance to thank you." Shipes has worked with a variety of people in the music industry and did not anticipate spontaneous displays of gratitude. It felt great. They caught up and made plans to meet again.

"Yo, next time you're in Cali, hit me," Hussle added. "I'll come out, scoop you." Hussle saw Shipes at LAX a few months later, picked him up in the Maybach, and drove him to the studio to listen to Victory Lap. "I've got to make sure I don't get choked up right here," Shipes adds as the memories come flooding back. "The last two years were identical to the first five." "Yo, come by the crib, come by the studio... " It was completely regular. Come by for Lauren's birthday. We're going to have a great time. That was probably simply his method of assuring me and him that everything was well.``

Hussle was great, deal or no deal. Because he held the rights to all of his mixtapes, he was making slightly under $1 million every quarter from streaming and downloads by the end of 2016. Before Victory Lap was even released, he uploaded his Tunecore royalty statement on Instagram, which totaled $908,312. "No flex," the caption said. "Only for motivational purposes." Controlling your catalogue is where the money is."

Nipsey Hussle chose to formalise this portion of his career in October 2016, announcing the creation of the Marathon Agency after years of making wise moves behind the scenes and pioneering unique methods to the entertainment industry. Hussle's godbrother Adam Andebrhan and longstanding Marathon partner Jorge Peniche were among the team's main members, as were two recognizable faces from Hussle's close circle—marketing and branding guru Karen Civil and rap industry A&R Steve Carless, who collaborated closely with Hussle on Victory Lap. Civil and Carless have known each other for a long time, having gone to the same high school in Elizabeth, New Jersey, and collaborating on YG and Jeezy ads. Hussle identified the Marathon Agency as "the new home for the RADICALS... in a social media post." THE REVOLUTIONARIES AND GAME-CHANGERS who believe they can do things their way."

Victory Lap's message included the fact that it was possible to escape the volcano alive. If Hussle could survive and prosper as a young man growing up in the Rollin' 60s, perhaps others can as well. "You can check the L.A. history," Hussle remarked. "My sector, in particular, is cannibalistic. You understand what I mean? They feed on their own. We don't have anyone who genuinely made it out of here. That was born and bred in this country. That person went to the booze stores. In the summer, I went swimming in the parks. They rode their bikes through these back alleys. Fought in the shadows of these structures. So the learning curve for the community, as well as the learning curve for myself, was really steep."

In this regard, the 1960s were hardly unique. Much of Los Angeles was ruled by gangs. When asked to describe the city's identity, Chuck Dizzle of Home Grown Radio paused before saying, "We're survivors—in every sense of the word." From the Watts Rebellion to the Rodney King Uprising, from police brutality to gangbanging, Los Angeles' neighbourhoods of colour have always been under attack. "There are families that actually feud because one is from one hood and the other is from the other," Dizzle explained. "The way Los Angeles is structured, this is one hood, this is another hood." You must coexist amicably. You've got to sort things out. There are youngsters who practically walk to school together—one side of the tracks is from here, and the other side is from there... They attend primary school together, and when they hop off the porch, which means they join a gang, they are compelled to choose a side. We were buddies. Now it's like—Aaaah, those were the days. And imagine if my relative is slain and I find out it was done by folks from your neighbourhood."

"That's how the streets are run in Los Angeles," Hustle explained. "Gangbangin'. I'm not hustlin'. You can be a successful hustler while having no say in the matter. You can have the bag and everything. It makes no difference, buddy. Niggas is going to take that away from you. True story. Because that is not the structure in Los Angeles. L.A.'s structure is on fire. So it's as if every village is run by a gang with a history. And got a story of what happened. And who did what, who sat down, who stood up, and who did what they were meant to do? And, as much as you are an individual, it is a way of life that your grandmother was aware of. Your aunts and uncles were aware of it. Everybody. The mailman understands the distinctions between the neighbourhoods in which he delivers mail."

Understanding the pervasiveness of gang culture opens us new avenues for reaching out to young people growing up in that context. Influences such as "gangsta rap" are an effect rather than a cause. "It's not like you wake up one day and say, 'Aw, that documentary inspired me.'" "I want to go bang," Hussle said. "Alternatively, 'I heard this record...' Or, 'I saw the video, and that's what I want to do.' Not to imply that other areas did not get it in the same way.Because everyone does what they do for a variety of reasons. But only as far as Los Angeles, the schoolteachers. It's the way of the streets, plain and simple. There's nothing alternative going on in the streets."

Creating alternatives to illegal hustling was a matter of survival, so when California voters adopted Proposition 64 in the November 2016 elections, legalising recreational marijuana usage, Hussle and his team jumped right in. There were benefits and drawbacks to legalising the marijuana trade. People who had endangered their freedom by selling cannabis to the public when it was illegal had a difficult time transitioning to the legal side of things. Because of his celebrity, Hussle had an edge. "I have a built-in marketing mechanism because I am an artist with fans and a platform," he explained. "So I didn't have the same challenges as someone who was just a hustler and was moving the packs." It's almost like a liquor licence. There are a limited number of licences available, and if you don't have a partner with one and can't get one yourself, you're out of luck. The same goes for cannabis. If you don't have a partner, there's no incentive for him to partner with you; he'll do it on his own."

Hussle and his crew selected the growth of a particular strain known as the Marathon OG after forming a collaboration with the Cure Company in California. He quickly started opening dispensaries to distribute the stuff. Using his celebrity to facilitate the legal cannabis deal, Hussle delegated day-to-day operations to his team, which included his childhood pal Stephen Donelson, also known as Bolt da Fatts. Fatts had grown up riding bikes around the neighbourhood with Nip and Sam, and was known for his devotion, winning smile, and can-do attitude. When Fatts and Nip joined the hood, they agreed that they would never fight each other. They'd been through a lot, from missions out of town with a burner hidden in the air conditioner to assisting Sam in selling apparel on the street before opening Slauson Tees.

"Fatts is a nigga who did a 180 in his life," Ralo explains. "He would be like the New Testament's Paul in that he was on his way to Damascus to kill Christians." And suddenly he was blinded by the light, and he turned around and became a disciple. "Do you get it?"In a nutshell, Fatts was family. Hussle thought that the new dispensaries would provide a consistent revenue stream while the All Money In team awaited the announcement of the record contract.

"Cannabis is a billion-dollar racket, though," Hustle explained, "so you gotta understand it's really aggressive and competitive." The question is, who will be Newport? Who will design the brand that will become the Newport or Marlboro of weed?"

As usual, Hussle's understanding of branding and corporate strategy was spot on. However, other forms of intense rivalry existed in the cannabis sector. And the area had witnessed different forms of arms races in the past. Fatts became the proprietor of Top Flight Collective, a cannabis dispensary with various sites, including one on West Boulevard at West Fifty-Ninth Place, just a few minutes from the Slauson and Crenshaw shopping plaza. During the fall of 2017, there was an attempted burglary at the location, according to sources in their 60s. "Whoever it is, whatever it is, if you've got somebody doing something that you want to do, you might be envious of it," one of the cast members explains. When Fatts and his colleagues looked into the attempted burglary, they wanted to discover if the offender was acting alone or if the effort was planned. "They handled it like the motherfuckers who were tutoring us would handle it," one

60s member adds. "They went out and did what they were supposed to do, and that's what landed 'em in the situation that drew all the attention to it all."

Fatts was standing in front of Top Flight Collective on the evening of September 29, 2017. He was hit by gunfire fired from a passing vehicle or vehicles at 10:45 p.m. Fatts dashed into the dispensary, fell, and died around 11:10 p.m. "They aired my nigga out," adds a knowledgeable neighborhood source who requested anonymity. "They shot him 30 times." It was terrifying. I'm not sure if I'm allowed to speak about what happened. It was a time of betrayal and brutality. I have no idea how the parade characters will play out or anything."There were two more dispensary shootings along Crenshaw around the same period, but no evidence linking them.

A impromptu monument of blue candles, blue and yellow flowers, and Mylar balloons flapping in the breeze quickly sprouted up on the sidewalk along the 5900 block of West Boulevard. Stephen J. Donelson's funeral was held at Calvary Baptist Church on Fairfax Avenue, immediately below Slauson. The thirty-year-old father was a cofounder and part owner of All Money In Records, The Marathon Clothing, and other shops in the plaza such as Wireless Connection and Baba Leo's Fish Shack, as well as Elite Human Hair, Fourth Ave Collective, and The Marathon OG, an exclusive strain developed by Hussle in collaboration with The Care Company. "You own 1/4 of everything I'm a part of," Hussle said on Instagram, beside a shot of blue and yellow candles arranged to read FATTS. "Ima make that worth 100 mill before we meet again," Leneice Patton wrote on his Los Angeles Times homicide report, which wrongly listed him as a hired security guard rather than the dispensary's owner. "My King, rest in Paradise... Sushi, I will always love you."

The loss upset Hussle and his immediate group. "Fatts, you know that's one of my best friends," he explained. "It was just a genuine friendship." And also one of those who truly believed that we could do something other than gangbang." It shook him to the core to lose a member of his day-one team just as their lifelong plans were coming to fulfilment. "I feel terrible that I'm the only one who just gets to feel it," Hussle remarked. "Fatts don't get to feel it."

A few months later, his feelings were still raw. When Elliott Wilson asked about Fatts, Hussle grew emotional near the end of his Rap Radar podcast interview. "Man, that completely caught me off guard," Hussle said. "I was completely unprepared for that. And the timing was off the charts. We've been sitting on everything. We've been holding our breath in order to accomplish it all at once. We've all been looking forward to this moment. And it's a little messed up—really messed up—that my partner and my homeboy aren't on this side of the dimension to experience and profit from it with us. And, you know, from..." He paused, wiping a tear from his eye, and cleared his voice. "I don't want to get too far into it." "I become emotional."

"I feel you," Wilson said in response. "Respect. Respect. Respect."

"But his kids, his kids, his kids would be proud of him."

Fatts is credited as an executive producer on Victory Lap's credits, and he should be. His contributions were critical to the successful completion of the All Money In mission. Nonetheless, his death overshadowed a significant triumph for the club, making the news of the Atlantic Records alliance in November 2017 somewhat bittersweet.

"The best day I ever had with Nip was when we got the Atlantic deal," Hussle's bodyguard J Roc stated. "Nip went the boss route and got what he wanted." And I was overjoyed."

"He said he couldn't be completely excited because Fatts wasn't here," said his Atlantic Records publicist Brittany Bell. "He felt bad celebrating such a moment because the person who had been there from the start was not present."

"I have regrets," Hussle admitted during one of his first interviews following the announcement of the contract. "I do. One of my homeboys died. And I think I may have stayed in the field too long. I may have taken too long to make this shift. At the same time, I shouldn't think that way, but I do. As in, dammit. How long did it take us to feel comfortable enough to pair up and make that next move?" He tried everything he could to turn the sorrow into inspiration. "We're gonna have to keep raisin' the value of what he's involved in, which is the music and the label."

In late November of 2017, Hussle and his crew officially announced their multimillion-dollar joint venture arrangement with Atlantic Records. He had done his homework and put his trust in the executive team, which included Craig Kallman as well as former Def Jam executives Julie Greenwald, Mike Kyser, and Kevin Liles, all of whom had established joint ventures such as Jay-Z's Roc-A-Fella Records and T.I.'s Grand Hustle. T.I. was imprisoned on federal firearms charges, and Atlantic shook with him as he rebuilt his career thereafter. "That's honourable," replied Hussle. "You don't seem to notice that." It didn't hurt that Hussle had known Dallas Martin, Atlantic's senior VP of A&R, since 2011, when he was at Warner Music alongside Rick Ross.

Despite living by the mantra "Fucc Tha Middleman" for years, Hussle was intrigued by the prospect of working with the legendary label that formerly housed Aretha Franklin and Ray Charles. It seemed that the sentiment was reciprocal. "He's really looked up to," Kallman remarked. "I believe he is a true icon, culturally significant to the entire West Coast." Victory Lap has piqued my interest. I think you've created a great album, and I can't wait to hear it."

"As kids, we always wished and hoped to be in that position, looking up at Snoop, Jay, Puff, and Master P doing things with music and being enterprising," Blacc Sam added. "And my brother was doing everything we had always admired other people doing." From the opening of the business to being featured in Forbes and GQ.

"We're finally getting the light shined back on us," Adam explained. "Because, you know, we've all been listening to the people of Atlanta." Even here in Los Angeles, we're drenched in southern culture. It's as if the light has returned to us, which hasn't happened in a long time."

After Hussle signed with Atlantic, everything began to move quickly. His crew noticed a difference immediately away. "He was just breaking down that wall of going to the real mainstream," DJ V.I.P. explains. "Not a mainstream sellout, but just a mainstream awareness." As Hussle's official tour DJ, V.I.P. watched crowds at his gigs grow by a factor of five to ten. "When that partnership evolved and began to grow, that's when we started doing larger festivals," he explained. Hussle would shortly appear on MTV's TRL and the BET Awards, as well as headline Broccoli Fest. "We'd seen some of these shows on smaller stages before," he explained. "But not the prime-time slots."

Hussle did not dabble with the mainstream. He and the All Money In squad jumped right in. Every door was open to them now that they were prepared. They'd soon sign deals with Puma and Jay-Z's management company, Roc Nation, throwing things into high gear. "We had Jay right there," V.I.P. claims. "Jay had never been so invested in a West Coast artist before." He had everyone on deck. He made his team and their assets completely available to us, and we were about to begin utilising them. That would have put us in nothing but arenas. We would have only done large tours, whether coheadlining or headlining. They simply have the resources to place you in those large places and sell out those seats."

Hustle and Boog headed to the Staples Center on Christmas Day 2017 to watch the Lakers face the Minnesota Timberwolves. Hussle was dressed in a Wilt Chamberlain throwback jersey and Lakers purple Puma suedes with gold stripes. The Lakers lost 121-104 despite youngster Kyle Kuzma's 31 points, but Hussle won. It was enough for him to be chilling courtside with his queen. They'd gone through a hard stretch in the previous month. He tweeted in late November about their decision to separate and focus on raising their children, then removed the comment. A few days later, his ex Tanisha, who was still known as Chyna Hussle on Twitter, tweeted about how they never broke up. Social media can really complicate life at times, especially when it comes to matters of the heart. Reality, however, always makes a reappearance sometime along the way, and Hussle and Boog were back on track relatively quickly.

The paparazzi flocked to their courtside flex at the Staples Center, and Hussle's choice of footwear was another clever chess move, previewing the Puma collaboration they would reveal on January 16, 2018. Hussle helped design the outfit, and the tracksuits looked like formal attire on his six-foot-three frame. Hustle wore the outfits on stage and during interviews. Puma sponsored his events and donated thousands of dollars to renovate the basketball court at 59th Street Elementary, which is across the street from his grandmother's house. Granny even got to drink champagne while flying.

NBA All-Star Weekend is more akin to a weeklong extravaganza involving some of the highest paid athletes in the world going absolutely ballistic. Additionally, it made for the ideal background for the Victory Lap rollout. Nipsey Hussle was undisputedly the ruler of Los Angeles for the entire week.

The only other contender for that reign was the prankster rapper from New York, Tekashi 6ix9ine, who boasted about not having to "check in" with any hoods while spending the whole All-Star week trolling social media with clever comments about L.A. gangs. The immensely popular singer was being blackmailed by members of his management team who were Nine Trey Gangsta Bloods associates; he would eventually testify against them in court in New York. In order to prevent reprisals, Tekashi cancelled all of his All-Star bookings and refrained from entering any hoods, but in spite of this, he amassed a sizable following on social media while poking fun at a tradition that Nipsey Hussle valued.

Hussle has a unique approach to dealing with individuals like Tekashi. To put them on "goofy time," he would simply ignore them until they destroyed themselves. When Tekashi Hussle was brought up in an interview, he always declined to comment, knowing that trolls ate up attention and that any mention of him would only help his career. Hussle did share some of his thoughts with his old pal DJ Drama during their conversation.

Drama remarked, "Tekashi is basically playing in the streets and getting a lot of attention." "What do you think about that?"

Hussle remarked, "I wouldn't speak to someone directly. "However, I wouldn't recommend doing what you mentioned about playing in the streets. I wouldn't join Atlanta's team. With New York, I wouldn't play. I won't play with any of them. 'Since there are real people everywhere, disrespecting someone's home will make them feel as though you were forcing their hand. Anywhere. Not just in LA.

Rappers frequently "check in" with a local gang before leaving town to ensure their safety. Hussle referred to the action as "friendly extortion," and he claimed that he preferred to move with respect instead. "I tap in and show respect when I come to Atlanta," he remarked. I don't live in my hometown. I put on my jewellery. If I don't walk and tread in the appropriate manner, I can become a victim. Despite our efforts to secure you, the program is bigger than you.

Hussle didn't even suggest that tourists who were in town for the All-Star festivities check in. He answered, "You can't pay me for no love." "I sell clothes, music, and various other drugs. I don't sell things like friendship or safety. However, it was a different story when it came to his true buddies. You're welcome to use my automobile, he said. You're welcome to visit my shop. Do you want to know where to eat? Meet my neighbourhood lads. You can find the numbers for niggas. Call in if there are any issues or anything else. That wasn't necessary for you to do. That is because there is power in numbers and we are all from the same location.

Three days before the album's release, on Tuesday, February 13, the identical Brinks truck from the "Hustle & Motivate" video came up in front of a Los Angeles strip club. All Money In emblems were now painted on the truck, which was now painted black. The back doors burst open, and Adam, Cowboy, J. Roc, Cobby, and Nipsey Hussle leaped out with hefty sacks of cash in each hand. They were all wearing AMI caps and black Victory Lap T-shirts. They shouted, "Neighbourhood!"

A TMZ reporter who was on the scene shouted, "Congratulations on the new album!" "What's going on with the armoured car?"

"All Cash In! That's the deal. Hussle bellowed. Nigga, bags. In charge of the baggage.

They went back to the neighbourhood and parked the All Money In Brink's truck near Crenshaw and Slauson after making it rain at the strip club that evening. Hussle soon began receiving calls. They had towed the truck. "Why?" Hussle questioned aloud. "What danger does this truck parked here pose?" He later learned that the truck was parked in a handicapped space and that the police had claimed the registration was invalid. But it was challenging to ignore the feeling that the LAPD was after him. He remarked, "We have a long and illustrious history with the Seventy-Seventh police department. They perceive success as a failure for them, to some extent... None of us are currently on probation or parole. We make large tax payments. We have a sizable local workforce. I'm confident that this corner's decreased crime rate is due to us. Four distinct apartments on Crenshaw and Slauson are rented out to us.

They took advantage of the circumstance by launching a raffle for a 14-karat gold pendant called All Money In. Hussle posted on Instagram, "Tha police buster ass towed our All Money In Brinks Truck," directing followers to go to the tow yard where the truck had been detained and take pictures with the hashtag #FREETHEBRINKSTRUCK. The receptionist at Pepe's Towing on Boyle Avenue reported, "We had a lot of people come down." It was between 300 and 400 niggas taking pictures in front of the gate, according to Hussle. "However, we didn't take it too seriously. We made light of it.

The following night, Hussle, J Stone, and BH partied on the streets of their city while dressed in a black du-rag, a white Puma Victory Lap tracksuit, and crazy gold chains. Hussle used the chance to talk about the cops even in the midst of the celebration over Victory Lap's publication. One thing that Hussle and his team don't respect is how the LAPD raided our Brink's truck. We perform for the city and demonstrate our affection. We are raising the standards for young Nigerians coming out of the hood. And we fail to comprehend why the cops would want to disparage that. But what's this? We're going to make a bad situation better. The Brink's truck has returned to Los Angeles. We now have possession of it again. We were there the entire All-Star weekend. Victory Lap is now formally retired.

Ralo discovered something odd about the guest appearances when he first had the chance to listen to the record in its entirety. On Victory Lap, "everybody's verse was paying homage to Nipsey," he claimed. Hip-hop is a sport with competition. Every time one rapper is asked to rhyme on another rapper's song, there is typically some subtle one-upmanship going on. (One extreme example is Kendrick Lamar's song-stealing guest verse on Big Sean's "Control"). Ralo remarked, "It's an honour to see that kind of garbage. "To have his debut record released, with such prominent features, and to have his contemporaries show such reverence for him. That thing was so strange. Like they were aware he would perish.

Hustle found time to officially open Vector90, the Crenshaw District coworking space, business incubator, and STEM academy that he co founded, amid the strip club parties and gold chain giveaways. At the inaugural event, his business partner David Gross, L.A. City Councilwoman Marqueece Harris-Dawson, and Don Peebles, a self-made Black billionaire who oversees $5 billion in real estate, were all present. Hussle claimed that the man was now constructing the highest skyscraper on the West Coast. And he is a success story from the first generation. That kind of achievement was amassed by his father, a mechanic, in just one generation.

Invited visitors and media explored the modern venue while listening to Victory Lap songs like "Grinding All My Life" and "Hussle & Motivate" while learning about an art display addressing the paucity of Black talent at high-tech corporations like Google and Facebook. To help close the distance between South Central and Silicon Valley, Vector90 was created.

It's a significant issue in Silicon Valley right now, according to Hussle. "There isn't enough diversity. It's because there aren't enough of our people in senior roles at these new, billion-dollar businesses. And when customers contact the corporations, the companies have an explanation. They claim there is no conduit connecting Silicon Valley's inner cities. Hussle recognized the impact such a resource could have as a young man who grew up in this community and was interested in technology.

He admitted, "I was never simply... a totally self-destructive young person. "I was always tinkering with computers, trying to learn how to build tracks, or trying to start rapping early. I almost gave up on attempting to be creative or to go against the grain of the culture I was surrounded by because I was so upset with having no outlet. I am aware of the strain that comes from having good intentions and then seeing that they are ineffective and saying, "Fuck it." Therefore, I believe that having those locations where individuals may connect early can save many people.

Desha Greene, one of the first businesspeople to use the space, remarked, "I grew up in this area and there is absolutely no space like this." The single mother of twins had to travel to coffee shops in order to arrange meetings while establishing her own dating app. She now had a place where she could work quietly and connect with other professionals who shared her interests. When the STEM academy opened, Greene intended to register her daughters there.

Later that evening, while Rance and the 1500 or Nothin' band warmed up the stage at the Hollywood Palladium, Hussle was backstage. There were many famous people present at the Victory Lap release party. Marsha Ambrosius joined Hussle onstage to play "Real Big" with him. Puffy was brought out to sing "Young Niggas." The renown Mozzy from Sacramento was brought out by him. He brought out J Stone, his childhood friend. The beat for "Last Time That I Checked" then began to be played by 1500 as a huge screen flashed the word VICTORY on a background that cycled between red and blue, and Hussle brought out... his daughter Emani.

Hussle declared, "That was my favourite guest of the night." She and I completed the set together. Emani, who was nine years old, grasped the mic while her father's voice played in the background. She was casually attired in a T-shirt and trousers and rapped the chorus with great authority. Evidently, she had remembered everything from those evenings spent in the studio. As his daughter finished her bars, Hussle placed an arm around her shoulders and gently led her to the side of the stage before YG stormed out to welcome his homeboy with a punch that could be felt all the way in the back of the auditorium. Their powerful display of solidarity during the show's finale sealed it with an explosive performance that will go down in L.A. rap history.

Hussle anticipated that the Victory Lap would mark the start of a completely new stage in his career. He admitted after the Victory Lap rollout, "I've learnt a lot by putting this out. "This is my first release on a major label. It's the first production that I've actually mixed and mastered. It's the first time we've truly carried out a comprehensive campaign, promoted an album, and done all of that. I think, "Cool, I got it." It was solved by me. I am familiar with every step. Everybody in the Atlantic I know. We have a track record. The following one must be larger. It must keep expanding.

Nip wanted a platinum album so he could charge platinum pricing since he was a hustler. But more than money, he desired to be respected as a man and as an artist. "People know the name Nipsey," he claimed. "They know he's from Los Angeles. In his city, he is well-liked. He's taken some action... However, I haven't really been able to flex that much musically. And this record served as a showcase for my progress in that approach. And I still have room to develop and space to simply show what I'm capable of.

# CHAPTER 6

## EXIT STRATEGY

Hussle stated, "I always had a political opinion," on a panel discussing mass incarceration and the prison industrial complex in January 2017. "I've always had some kind of comprehension. Nobody is interested in your viewpoint, though, until I have a voice and a solid reputation as a successful artist. It is meaningless. People judge your perspective based on how far it has brought you rather than looking at the car you're coming up in, where you live, or your financial situation.

Nip had come a long way in his three decades on earth according to his own particular ideology. He had been derided for most of his life as a Rollin' 60s Crip and a "gangsta rapper," but now he had earned the right to participate in a public discussion with an Oscar-nominated director, a professor from California State University, a police commissioner from Los Angeles, a lawyer, and a CNN contributor. Nipsey Hussle was accurately described as a "business mogul, philanthropist, and community activist" on the event flyer for the screening of Ava DuVernay's enlightening documentary 13th.

Nipsey would never downplay the difficult journey he had taken or the challenges he had faced in order to reach this stage, in keeping with his Marathon mindset. "If you're a young Black or Latino male, going to jail is just something you expect to happen in your life," Nipsey said. "The movie gave words to something that we young people instinctively felt and understood. We don't necessarily have the breakdown of the facts, but we believed that this needed to be set up. This can't all be coincidence, you know. There has to be a plan behind this.

Nipsey continued by sharing a recent event from his own life as an example. He announced, "I've got a few businesses on Crenshaw and Slauson, in the actual strip mall right there," to the cheers of the audience. "I wasn't bragging," he clarified. I wished to emphasise a point.

Before he could continue, one of the audience members shared his personal testimony due to Hussle's approachable relatability.

Someone yelled from somewhere in the room, "That's what we need!" That is what we require! more companies. more reliable companies that prioritise Black people."

"No question," Nipsey answered.

The brother continued, his voice growing louder, "'Cause all they people want is money!"

Nip acknowledged him by saying, "Yeah," allowing him to express himself.

"You all have bread. Make it happen! similar to what you did at Slauson and Crenshaw. He likely wasn't thinking of the panellists when he said "y'all," but rather other Black people. those who had not attended this community dialogue.

Of course," Hussle replied.

The voice from the audience replied, "We need real, tangible results. "Our protest needs to catch up to physical labour. You can't just march and then go home without anyone pooling their resources to make any purchases.

Hussle bowed to the man's urgent message and answered, "Right," giving up his position.

The man said, down to the decimal, "The population of Los Angeles: 4.7 million white, 4.2 million Latino, and 800,000 Black," as if he knew the numbers all too well. "Nowhere will rent a room to a Black man!"

"Right," replied Hussle.

The audience member's voice was now harrowing with emotion. Witnessing a brief moment of public catharsis, the audience, the moderator, and the other panellists sat in silence.

The man said, "I can't rent a room because none of my people don't own no fuckin' homes!" Real estate is as real as it gets. Even in one of Los Angeles's oldest Black neighbourhoods, which had been severely damaged by gentrification and disinvestment, it was challenging to find a place to call home.

Nipsey reacted by saying, "Real shit," confirming the sincerity of the anguish being expressed. True sh*t. You make a valid point, I agree. As he continued his own testimony, the air in the room appeared to start to return.

"The reason I brought it up," Hussle recalled, "was I was in that parking lot just passing by, and one of my people contacted me like, 'Bro, police over here has somebody hemmed up. Calm down. I then kicked it for five minutes at the gas station. Then he gave it some more thinking. "I'm not on probation," he declared. "I don't squat."

The audience responded by bursting out in tight laughter as they related to the emotion.

Nipsey continued, "So I drove in." "The police pulled me over as I was driving in the parking lot," I said. He had gone through the ritual so frequently that he started joking around with the officers.

He said, "I let 'em do their thing. They said, "Yeah, bro, I just wanna give you a heads up,' as they were getting ready to go. One of the top 10 gang targets in Los Angeles, according to the city attorney, is your store.

There was a general grumble from the audience.

"So I'm wondering, 'Why is that?'" And we've only begun to converse. Hussle was back in the present as he spoke, restating his argument to a more receptive audience.

The first is that starting a business and succeeding in it is extremely, very difficult, he remarked. "Especially if you don't come from successful business owners," The audience cheered in unison. "So, we previously addressed that. And we handled that without any assistance from you all.Second, everyone who works at this store is a local," he said. And might contribute to your problem if it weren't for this store. This time, the applause was louder.

In reference to a $3 billion light rail project from LAX, Hussle said, "Number three, they're doing a big development on Crenshaw." They are building all kinds of things. Only when we do it is it a problem, right? The audience was now completely exposed. What will happen if a Shell gas station, a Hungry Harold's, or any of these companies are built? Hussle enquired. "Is that not a hangout for gangs?"

Hussle knew from experience that regardless of their actual character or intentions, any man, woman, or child from this neighbourhood might perhaps be labelled as a gang member, linked with a gang, or "from a gang area" in the eyes of the LAPD. Gang injunctions—and the ideas that led to them—were still very much in effect as the ACLU's federal complaint worked its way through the legal system.

Hussle told the cops that their goals were to "protect and serve," which was written on the door of every police vehicle, and that "your interests are not in conflict with ours." As business owners, "we have a similar interest," he continued. The policeman in the parking lot assured him that the city attorney's viewpoint would change if they heard him speak.

Hussle complained to the audience, "But we don't get to speak." "We find a case, they arrive to shut us down, and we face reality. We deal with debts that need to be paid, overhead costs that are still present, and the closure of our legal activity.The cycle has repeated itself several times. What was Hussle's plan of escape? Would he be able to change the pattern and move from surviving to thriving?

Hussle stayed in marathon mode despite all the failures, ready to bounce back and give it another shot. "I know our generation, we got tired of trying," he said. "Or even observing others try and fail. In terms of culture, there are no Black Panther organisations. The closest thing is Black Lives Matter. Previously, that served as a young person's vent for frustration.

He then said, "And now?" You have gangs. Because Niggas said, "Fuck it," he is now gangbangin'. when you grow weary of merely trying to do what is right while feeling burdened by the weight of an uphill struggle to accomplish what is right.

But perhaps it was now time to give it another shot.

A positive step was taken by initiatives like this panel discussion. bringing together academics, professionals, and families to examine Black past in an effort to map out the future. The public was able to address the ways that corporate interests and public policies have worked together to maintain the heritage of slavery through seeing and discussing 13th, which DuVernay created. Viewers were also inspired to come up with solutions to end these cycles.

How long does a moment exist before it transforms into a movement? questioned DuVernay. She discussed the stirring impact of the horrible killing of Emmett Till, a fourteen-year-old Chicago boy travelling to Mississippi to visit family in 1955. He allegedly upset a white woman named Carolyn Bryant while passing by a grocery store; Bryant would later admit that she made up some of the specifics of her tale. Emmett Till was kidnapped by Bryant's husband and his half brother from the house of his great-uncle. The youngster was beaten, shot, had barbed wire wrapped around his neck, was fastened to a huge metal fan, and finally had his body lowered into the Tallahatchie River. His body was discovered three days later and brought back to Chicago, where his mother Mamie insisted on an open-casket funeral. Many people came to see Emmett Till's deformed body, which was even captured on camera while his mother was present for Jet magazine. Rapidly, a white jury exonerated Till's murderers. The boy's lynching sparked outrage, which fueled the Civil Rights movement. Rosa Parks and Martin Luther King Jr. became well-known later that year thanks to the Montgomery Bus Boycott.

According to DuVernay, Trayvon Martin served as the equivalent of Emmett Till in terms of a genuine outcry that sparked action. "Unfortunately, we've been fed a continual diet of horror, dread, and trauma that kept us from being able to rage against it. We have organised to combat it. And now we have a president who, in my opinion, isn't really doing anything novel. Simply speaking out loudly and discussing it on Twitter, he.

Dr. Melina Abdullah remarked, "When we talk about the history of our Black liberation movement, we resisted from the moment we were taken from the shores of Africa, as Angela mentioned. The cofounder of the Los Angeles chapter of Black Lives Matter and chair of Pan-African Studies at Cal State University, Los Angeles, spoke on the contribution of the Black Arts movement to the fight. We need our artists to understand their roles, as W. E. B. DuBois once stated, quoting poets Amiri Baraka and Sonia Sanchez.

The panel's moderator advised Hussle to exercise caution. "You might have to rap that song I like."11

He grinned as he stated, "She talkin' about this record called 'Fuck Donald Trump,'" as the audience erupted in cheers. According to Hussle, movies like 13th aid in the historical reconstitution of his generation. "You might have an understanding of one of the issues," he added, "which was the increase in incarceration over the decades." Hussle gained self-assurance after learning more about the political processes and commercial objectives underlying the prison industrial complex.

Hussle was gathering the resources to voice his opinions and ensure that people were paying attention after the summer 2017 opening of The Marathon Clothing smart store, which paved the stage for the release of Victory Lap. Not just music, though. At a time when many Black-owned businesses were being priced out by investors who were getting ready for the advent of the light rail and the football stadium being built in Inglewood, he was starting businesses and creating jobs. He was collaborating with the Los Angeles City Council on a public arts initiative called Destination Crenshaw to help halt the gentrification-related process of cultural oblivion. Someone needed to provide affordable homes in the neighbourhood in order to truly help folks like the man who raised his hand during the panel discussion. There was a lot to accomplish and not nearly enough time.

Tick-tick-tick.

David Gross's 24-year-old brother Sean Mack was killed in Inglewood on July 7, 2017. "My younger brother was born after I left L.A., and we developed our relationship from afar," recalled Gross. "When I returned to Los Angeles, we grew quite close. He was my employee, and we were close friends. A Blood set member and wannabe rapper, Sean Mack. Defining his younger brother as "just a really cool, dynamic, and charismatic kid," Gross said.

Gross stated, "I wish I could turn back the hands of time and show my older brother something else. "He wouldn't currently be imprisoned. I wish I had been able to seize my little brother and present him with an alternative scenario. He wouldn't currently be in a grave, would he?

Oakland, Chicago, Detroit, Baltimore, Philadelphia, Atlanta, and Memphis were among the Black metropolises in America that Gross and Hussle hoped would spark a revolution. I don't know where the concept of buying back the block came from, but it has permeated our culture, said Gross. "Nipsey spent his entire career preaching and rapping about black greatness and ownership. We reasoned that having lots of the people that moved culture would be the fastest way to change the thinking, which would then change the culture. What T.I. is to Atlanta, Meek Mill is to Philadelphia, and Nip is to South Central. Imagine if they were all collaborating to achieve a single objective.

However, his vision wasn't made up in any way. It was already in motion, and Hussle was undoubtedly a key factor. Hip-hop had grown to be significant and influential enough that it made sense for groups of artists to unite and ensure that they were working for their best interests, much like the NBA has a players' organisation. Although Roc Nation served as a shining example of what was possible, much more work remained.

Hussle stated to Fader in January 2017 that "we have to leave the door open when somebody gets in." "We have to handle this crap properly. That's why YG and I came here after seeing what happened with Death Row. Because the street politics couldn't last very long, they failed. Therefore, as leaders, YG and I had to ensure that it was done correctly from an L.A. viewpoint, despite the fact that YG is a Blood and I am on the Crip side. I screw with Meek Mill and hip-hop in general. Only yesterday were we seated at the table. Drake, Meek, T.IJ Prince, Mustard, and others were seated at the table while those chats took place, demonstrating the type of dialogues that were taking place. If niggas actually do it the right way, it's almost like some Corleone, Five Families crap. We may certainly approach it from the perspective of a player's association and ensure fairness.

Hussle was experimenting with new business ideas now that he had cracked the music industry's code. The young person who constructed his own computer and created his own beats naturally moved on to other areas of technology.

He declared, "I want to really get into tech." "I have some concepts about which I am really enthusiastic. It reminds me a lot of how I used to view hip hop, and I'm sure I could be useful. I want to set up the meetings and have the conversations about that using my platform as an artist and as someone who is well-known in the music industry. I'll merely exercise due vigilance and continue to learn. Silicon Valley and Los Angeles were only separated by a large conceptual chasm and a single flight of an hour. Hussle maintained, "We were supposed to be involved. "When we were growing up, there were no computers, and then there were computers. You get me? And I saw how getting Pro Tools and getting a computer revolutionised my life. And I had a significant impact on my life by learning how to engineer my own recordings. I want to participate in that.

Hussle observed how heavily the major tech corporations relied on hip-hop, the most popular musical genre on streaming services at the time. According to Hussle, "Dr. Dre was one of the pioneers in that space with the streaming service that evolved into Apple Music, as well as the hardware, the headphones." "Any one of these billion-dollar platforms derives a significant portion of its value from the influential users. And none of those folks ever work for the company. However, they are making use of the attention they attract.

At Lakers games, Hussle frequently encountered unusual individuals. The people seated next to him at the Staples Center were typically interesting to talk to because he had good seats. Sean Rad, the creator of Tinder, who was sitting next to him at one game, explained how an app is valued. Hussle stated, "He told me an equation." In essence, every app user is charged a fixed sum of money. The value of your firm is based on users times this sum of money if you wish to sell your software. You may determine the company's valuation by adding up all of the users on Twitter who have 10 million followers. Hussle noted that the concept is an attention- and eyeball-based revenue model when Twitter is valued at so-and-so billion. "And why are they paying attention, exactly? a famous person. the creator.

Hussle lived by rules and ideals that included giving back to the community since he felt responsible for it. The fundamental rules cannot be broken, he admonished. "Stay true to what you say. Follow through on your promises. Treat others with respect, just as you would want to be treated. He never lost sight of the fact that Jay-Z did not introduce him to the game. It was the individuals who purchased his mix CDs for $5 when he was positioned in the plaza at Slauson and Crenshaw. He said, decades later, "People supported me when they didn't have a reason to." They said, "You know what?" "I commend your ambition as a young person trying."

Despite their growing popularity, All Money In and the Marathon name remained a family-run enterprise. Hussle stated, "My dad works for The Marathon Clothing. He works at the shop every day.

My business partner is my brother. We cowork with my sister. Moms. Everybody." Hussle felt a sense of family among the main team members as well as the community that helped to support the enterprise as a whole. He never seemed to be discouraged by the fact that the neighbourhood was entangled with a complex gang hierarchy that had its own set of internal politics.

Hussle declared that they are all legitimate companies with staff members. "That requires management and commitment from everyone. Everyone is dedicated to my dream, so I do feel accountable.

Nipsey Hussle was not only a singer, businessman, and activist; he was also a pioneer. He developed novel answers to old problems by always searching out new information and sharing it with the world. He was experimenting at Vector90 with different means of deriving value from the community's knowledge base in addition to financial rewards. People could receive credit to use the coworking space above by volunteering to share their knowledge at the STEM academy located downstairs. People's greatest desire was cultural experience; it served as their actual source of inspiration. "You can inspire someone to the point where they work for the movement if you focus and zero in," he remarked. "You sowed a seed in 'em. When they enter a room, they feel as though they have the chance to impress nine people by giving them drugs if there are nine persons in the room who are unaware of them. His emphasis on quality rather than quantity was ultimately paying dividends.

To be the best version of Nipsey Hussle was the task at hand. to live up to and represent everything that meant something to the world. We serve as an inspiration, he claimed. "I believe we stand for staying down. We exemplify lifting yourself up by your bootstraps, in my opinion. We, in my opinion, stand for one of the fundamental tenets of hip-hop. Staying true to the land was a crucial part of that. "I started on Crenshaw and Slauson," he declared. "I'm currently at Crenshaw & Slauson. The Marathon is still on.

It took Hussle ten years to release his debut album. He wasn't attempting to spend any more time now that he had his situation organised and was putting the finishing touches on yet another recording studio, this time with the most cutting-edge equipment in a secure area.

Once or twice a week, Nip and I would text each other, claims Ralo. He sent me images of the new studio and pursued me aggressively. Recently, he had agreed to a ten-year lease for an entire floor in the structure where they had finished Crenshaw. "He was having showers installed, and there was an SSL board and at least five or six different studio rooms that had been built out with the bass traps, mixing consoles, and vocal booths—everything's professional, the lighting was dope as fuck." Hussle wished for Ralo to return and commit to the All Money In production. Hussle said, "Look, we're going to work till you need a break. We won't exhaust ourselves by being with one another. After receiving what we sought, we will continue with our business.

Hussle's plan didn't end with the release of Victory Lap. The objective, he continued, "was to get the record out, but we had a detailed strategy of what we wanted to do, so getting the label extremely solid is part of that. He has Killa Twan, Pacman, J Stone, Cobby, and BH on his upcoming All Money In album. "We gon' come with the original home team of my homies that grew up in the section with us and built the sound with us," Hussle declared. It would be a return to group music-making, which is how they all got started, but on a totally different level.

Hussle said to DJ Drama, "I'm getting ready to start recording again for the next one." "I'm attempting to return right away. We need to get gas because it took me so long to make my formal debut. The topic is music. I have a clear plan for how I want to deliver the albums covered by this contract. I want a focused window to complete this. I don't want to take a two-year break and do nothing.

Hussle stated, "I have an album concept called Exit Strategy, and that might be one of my last ones. It's a phrase used in commerce while forming corporations. As you build a business, you develop your exit strategy. Don't wait until you've been doing it for five years. So, going public or selling are two common exit strategies for businesses. The premise that any brand peaks during a specific time window served as the foundation for the concept. "You have a window of opportunity as an artist, a brand, a rapper, or a musician, but many people—even athletes—don't have an exit strategy. Living in the delusion that things will always be this way is all that it is. Everything, including their manner of life and financial habits. I have a plan B in case I don't feel like moving in that manner.

It was crucial to know when to stop playing or working—in music, business, and the stock market. If you give up while you're ahead, it's not considered quitting, he said. It comes down to being alert and strategic enough to realise that you must eventually exit the pool. You must dry off and put on your old clothing.

Hussle talked about being "Stuck In The Grind" on No Pressure, a collaboration mixtape he made with a budding musician named Bino Rideaux and released on November 25, 2017. Naturally, he would rap on Victory Lap about "Grinding All My Life." In an official music video, Hussle mixed the two songs to highlight the tenacity of his work ethic. He frequently talked about working extra hard while the celebrity was glowing in order to have enough to support his family when that light started to wane.

Hussle thought he had another fifty songs in the stockpile when Victory Lap was published. "I got the album done, like mastered in my hand," he declared. "Okay, what are we going to do next? We need to record some films, market the project, and plan the release. In music mode, please. We have a ton of music, that's for sure. He and Bino worked together on at least two other projects. He has the

Future album, which featured James Fauntleroy, Daz Dillinger, and Hi-Tek on the beat. He had also joined Meek Mill in the recording studio. There was also the Cardi B song. Hussle and his daughter were both fans of Cardi's music, despite a little internet uproar when Hussle questioned her choice to use vulgar gang language on social media. First of all, Hussle noted, "She's a woman." "That's not what I do; I'm not even into addressing women in any manner other than with love and respect."

More significantly, they had entered the studio and worked with producer Lil' C on a song called "I Just Wanna Know' ' that featured a rhythm by Mars from 1500. It is a banger, he declared. It's an anthem to fuck. Mike Will was tasked by Hussle with polishing the production and adding a little additional zing. Hussle remarked, "She kilted the verse. "Can a Crip nigga fuck with a Blood bitch?" is what she asks in her verse. Hussle and YG's message of unity was elevated significantly by the song. Hussle expressed his desire for it to be released. Additionally, he had been recording with Roddy Rich, a fresh L.A. talent whom Dallas Martin had come across.

Hussle had no idea which songs would be included on which project, but he understood how he wanted to wrap everything up. When our collaboration with Atlantic is resolved, I'm going to call my final album The Spook Who Sat by the Door, he declared. If you haven't watched the movie or read the book, it's about a Chicago gang member who pretended to be someone else. He never made any arrests. He had a neat appearance. He also snuck into the CIA. He acquired knowledge, and in essence he exploited their plan—to have a symbolic nigga in the CIA for political purposes—against them.

Hussle wasn't exactly a straight-laced agent of the CIA like Dan Freeman, the antihero of The Spook Who Sat by the Door, who melted into the background. Because he knew who he intended to mobilise, he added, "that's one of the reasons I was so vocal about where I was coming from and where I represented." Hussle performed the role of the typical "gangsta rapper," but with a completely different goal, distinguishing hip-hop culture from "the power structure of the music industry." Hussle claimed, "They got the personas they were expecting from us." Therefore, I believe that one of my fundamental methods was the way he used their intention against them.

Charlamagne Tha God of The Breakfast Club, who recognized the Spook allusion in "Blue Laces 2" since he had read the book and watched the movie, added, "You gotta put the medicine in the candy." What's noteworthy about that book is how everyone who knew him referred to him as an Uncle Tom, a coon, and a sellout. He added, "And he was there the entire time working for them. "You sowed a seed in 'em. When they enter a room, they feel as though they have the chance to impress nine people by giving them drugs if there are nine persons in the room who are unaware of them. His emphasis on quality rather than quantity was ultimately paying dividends.

To be the best version of Nipsey Hussle was the task at hand. to live up to and represent everything that meant something to the world. We serve as an inspiration, he claimed. "I believe we stand for staying down. We exemplify lifting yourself up by your bootstraps, in my opinion. We, in my opinion, stand for one of the fundamental tenets of hip-hop. Staying true to the land was a crucial part of that. "I started on Crenshaw and Slauson," he declared. "I'm currently at Crenshaw & Slauson. The Marathon is still on.

It took Hussle ten years to release his debut album. He wasn't attempting to spend any more time now that he had his situation organised and was putting the finishing touches on yet another recording studio, this time with the most cutting-edge equipment in a secure area.

Once or twice a week, Nip and I would text each other, claims Ralo. He sent me images of the new studio and pursued me aggressively. Recently, he had agreed to a ten-year lease for an entire floor in the structure where they had finished Crenshaw. "He was having showers installed, and there was an SSL board and at least five or six different studio rooms that had been built out with the bass traps, mixing consoles, and vocal booths—everything's professional, the lighting was dope as fuck." Hussle wished for Ralo to return and commit to the All Money In production. Hussle said, "Look, we're going to work till you need a break. We won't exhaust ourselves by being with one another. After receiving what we sought, we will continue with our business.

Hussle's plan didn't end with the release of Victory Lap. The objective, he continued, "was to get the record out, but we had a detailed strategy of what we wanted to do, so getting the label extremely solid is part of that. He has Killa Twan, Pacman, J Stone, Cobby, and BH on his upcoming All Money In album. "We gon' come with the original home team of my homies that grew up in the section with us and built the sound with us," Hussle declared. It would be a return to group music-making, which is how they all got started, but on a totally different level.

Hussle said to DJ Drama, "I'm getting ready to start recording again for the next one." "I'm attempting to return right away. We need to get gas because it took me so long to make my formal debut. The topic is music. I have a clear plan for how I want to deliver the albums covered by this contract. I want a focused window to complete this. I don't want to take a two-year break and do nothing.

Hussle stated, "I have an album concept called Exit Strategy, and that might be one of my last ones. It's a phrase used in commerce while forming corporations. As you build a business, you develop your exit strategy. Don't wait until you've been doing it for five years. So, going public or selling are two common exit strategies for businesses. The premise that any brand peaks during a specific time window served as the foundation for the concept. "You have a window of opportunity as an artist, a brand, a rapper, or a musician, but many people—even athletes—don't have an exit strategy. Living in the delusion that things will always be this way is all that it is. Everything, including their manner of life and financial habits. I have a plan B in case I don't feel like moving in that manner.

Hussle responded, "I don't wanna blow anything up like he did in the movie. But even just being able to rally his friends for a greater good is something I think we all need to accomplish. In his song "Dedication," Kendrick mentions it. At the Pac premiere, Kendrick, Top, and I had a conversation with Snoop and Kendrick. Just a little bit of what we are discussing.

Hussle's escape plan was going exactly as planned. He only required a little bit more time. Hussle visited the KRRL FM radio station for one of his final interviews, and Big Boy questioned him about how much of his iceberg was visible above the surface. Hussle responded, "For serious, I'd say just the tip of the iceberg. "Considering how long we've been pushing and how much ground we've covered, it's crazy. The entire time, I was playing at a disadvantage. I have been claiming to have been paid to actually practise. I have no idea how to accomplish anything. Our training was on the job. And to be standing where I am right now? use the knowledge, resources, and connections I possess. If only we were still standing there, we could do what we did. And what can we do here?

On Slauson and Crenshaw in the late afternoon of September 14, 2018, Blacc Sam was faced with a potentially fatal circumstance. In the parking lot of the shopping centre, shots were fired. A Rollin' 60s member had entered Marathon Clothing in search of trouble when a brawl started.

Blood was on the ground when police arrived. All of the on-scene witnesses were, at best, uncooperative. A man who required nine staples in his head after being severely battered and stabbed was interviewed by police. He stated that Blacc Sam had hit him with a metal pipe and assaulted him, but he remained silent when pressed about how the fight had begun. Despite the fact that several witnesses reported hearing gunshots, he denied that any firearms had been used or even that there had been a shooting. The "victim" was shown on camera pulling something out of the glove box as she approached the store after arriving in a red car. A little while later, he can be seen bleeding and running back to the car while being pursued by an unidentified group of people.

Blacc Sam was detained for a month after being arrested for assault despite the contrary evidence. At the time, Rihanna was hosting her fourth annual Diamond Ball at Cipriani Wall Street, and Hussle was three thousand miles away. "Honestly, bro, that situation was just a case of the police just being' devilish," Hussle added. "They observe our actions. They can make out the energy. They can see the path we are taking. They still despise our past and where we came from. They thus seize opportunities. E. Y. Song, who oversaw the shopping centre for its owners in the wake of the incident, filed an eviction petition in an effort to have all of the Asghedom brothers' establishments, including the Marathon Clothing smart store, removed.

Sam secured his own $1 million bond and appeared in court a month after his arrest, when his charges were dropped. According to other evidence and claims from unnamed witnesses, "the victim's account is somewhat contradicted," said Alice Kurs of the Los Angeles District Attorney's Office. The group of guys may have hit the victim in self-defence (or to take the pistol away from him) if the victims had arrived at the scene armed and ready to engage the suspect. Hussle and his brother travelled to Las Vegas with their grandma on the Puma private aircraft for a charity event where they distributed sneakers to high school students. On his approach to the jet, Sam said, "You know I gotta talk some shit." "A $1,000,000 bond. What are you talking about, Nigga? We are already in Vegas.

BH was carefree as he rode in Hussle's Maybach through South Los Angeles. The young apprentice of Nip stated, "Our hood went through some insane sh*t in the last twenty or thirty years. "It kind of looked like a dark cloud over our entire neighbourhood." He had made the decision to abandon his previous way of life after being shot. He claims, "It ain't even worth it." "I nearly died. And for what did I nearly pass away? Nothing!"

He would frequently discuss with Nip how to improve conditions for the children that would follow them. Hussle would often declare, "It's not about us anymore. "Hogg, let's inspire 'em. Just let's keep going! These students need to be inspired to know where they can also engage in this behaviour. They do not need to walk the streets. They can emulate us and say things like, "Damn, that nigga successful!" However, they are from nowhere! They're from the neighbourhood, but they're doing things their way.

Hussle remained grounded at Crenshaw and Slauson for that reason. He was attempting to improve this stuff, claims BH. Nip has already begun opening all the businesses. But one thing I used to often say to Nip was, "Bro, get the fuck from over here, bro! Now that we have these businesses and shit established!" Don't even come over here like that, please.Because we have already completed our work. They are already aware that it is our garbage.

BH will always remember his final exchange with Hussle. He came to collect me, and we just chatted while driving.

"BH, you made it hard on yourself," Hussle remarked.

"What do you mean?" BH answered.

He said, "Bro, all you do is drive Lambos and Rolls-Royces." "You can't turn around now—boy, you have to keep moving! But you can do it, nigga; I know it. Keep on, my brother! Now, you are unable to go back. As they drove through South Central's streets, they started to laugh. In the distance, you could see the city's illuminations. Hussle said, "One more thing," to him. "What you gotta understand too, bro, is that the hood looks at you like a mirror—and looks at me like a mirror."

"What do you mean by that, bro?" BH enquired of him.

He asserted that the neighbourhood's animosity toward us was not the cause. "The people over here all have the same dreams, but nobody has succeeded in realising those dreams. They failed to achieve their objectives. As a result, they are now angry with us because they see us in a mirror as we drive down Slauson in the Maybach, Rolls-Royce, or whatever the hell it is. Considering that we succeeded in doing what they failed to do. BH said to me, "I still feel what he was saying, today."

# CHAPTER 7

# TOO BIG TO FAIL

"Don't deceive!" In front of "the amazing Nipsey Hussle the Great" on the GQ Couples Quiz set, Lauren London reprimanded her guy. Hussle replied with a smile, sitting forward in his director's chair against a backdrop of gentle pastel hues, "I was just looking down at my jewellery," I did not pay attention to the questions.

London clutched thirty index cards in her hands, each bearing a question meant to gauge how well her true love knew her. Hussle accepted the challenge with a spirit of fun competition, unfazed by the pressure of being subjected to such an intimate grilling by his significant other—on camera, no less. Lauren replied with a sweetly adoring tone, "See, he stays ready, so he doesn't have to get ready.

"You've got the script down!" Hussle responded admiringly. It shouldn't have surprised anyone. When you fall in love with an actress, that is what occurs.

The XXL editor who placed Hussle on the cover in 2010 said of him, "This was a man who was proud to be with his woman," Vanessa Satten. Many rappers are pleased to have lots of ladies, as you can see. The timing of that stunning fashion photo featuring Nipsey and Lauren together was especially heartbreaking because their relationship appeared to be based on true love.

The endearing eight-minute short, which was published on March 28, 2019, one month after Hussle and Boog's epic GQ feature debuted, saw roughly 15 million views in only one year. It quickly turned into one of those instances that seems destined to last as long as YouTube does. Even though you are aware that the most romantic love stories rarely have a happy ending, there is an uncontrollable delight in witnessing two people who are so in sync chat with one another.

Where did we initially meet?At my store, on Crenshaw and Slauson.What impression did I have of you?She was completely sprung.

I misspoke and said, "I thought he was very tall."

In his GQ feature of the pair, Mark Anthony Green stated that "Nipsey Hussle and Lauren London occupy the same branch on the pop-culture tree in terms of their careers." The branch that White America hasn't yet fully exploited is what I refer to as. It has benefits and drawbacks.

Autonomy, genuineness, and magnificence are obvious advantages. Once you are able to decipher the matrix (the entire matrix, from the Spook Hunters to the Proud Boys—not to mention the prison industrial complex and the music industrial complex) and come up with a plan to stop the exploitation machinery, dealing with the cons may become simpler. After pulling off that incredible feat, Hussle became more likely to criticise CEOs than other rappers. On the Victory Lap album's title track, he bragged, "I'm integrated vertically, y'all niggas blew it," confident in the knowledge that he owned not only the rights to all of his raps but also the means of delivery—The Marathon Clothing smart store.

The slogan "Too Big to Fail," which became well-known during the financial crisis of the late 2000s to justify government bailouts of failed Wall Street corporations using taxpayer money, was borrowed by Hussle and David Gross when they gave the STEM centre at Vector90 the name. As Federal Reserve Chair Ben Bernanke put it, "a too-big-to-fail firm is one whose size, complexity, interconnectedness, and critical functions are such that, should the firm go unexpectedly into liquidation, the rest of the financial system and the economy would face severe adverse consequences." Hustle and Gross were asserting that people may be just as significant as financial organisations by reclaiming that phrase and using it to refer to South Los Angeles populations. They had the hubris to imply that the residents of this particular neighbourhood were too significant and interwoven to allow them to fail.

Hussle ran over to Puerto Nuevo Coffee on West Slauson on Saturday, March 30, to pick up some green juice. He always wanted to make the most of his time with his family, so he took Emani with him. He frequently asked, "Do you know how kids spell love?" "T-I-M-E." Finding personal time was a regular struggle because of his numerous enterprises, studio sessions, video shoots, and promos. That's not an easy task, he remarked. But it's worthwhile because you're extending your presence here, therefore it's worth it. You continue to leave a legacy. It won't be one-sided, I promise. You receive a benefit from that.

Hussle drove Emani to school every day, unless he was out of town, and he tried to make the most of their time together. When Hussle and NBA player and devoted parent Stephen Curry were sharing thoughts on fatherhood, Hussle once quipped, "We have a little convo before she gets out of the car." Hussle grinned as he remarked, "She gets sick of me runnin' the script, but I pound it in her head."

"What exactly is integrity?"

Being honest means acting morally even when no one is watching.

Okay, are you a follower or a leader?

I am a boss.

What makes a difference?

Think independently.

"Okay, do you feel confident?"

Yes.

"What is faith?"

Have faith in myself.

That's our morning routine, he said. "I want her to reflect back on the things I thought were significant when she gets older, even though it seems simple. everything my father instilled in me from a young age: leadership, self-assurance, and honesty. Even if she isn't able to fully accept these concepts just yet, she won't be able to forget them when she is older and has the opportunity to reflect on the direct message I was trying to convey. My father believed that having honesty, leadership, and confidence was extremely important.

Someone attempted to walk past Hussle as he and Emani sat at the counter of Puerto Nuevo's modest coffee shop waiting for his freshly squeezed juice.

"What's up, Nip?"

When he turned around, a face he hadn't seen in a while greeted him.

"Your name is Firebug, huh?" said Nip.

Yes, the man answered. He was around Nip's age and height, a little more musclebound, with short hair and a well-kempt beard. His tattoos revealed his allegiance. His facial expression conveys strength and humility.

Nips grinned. "You're from Centinela Park?"

"Yeah."

East Inglewood's Centinela Park Family is a Blood group that shares territory with the Rollin' 60s. The competing sets have been savage rivals for years. The story of Nipsey's set versus Centinela going back-to-back-to-back is told in the song "Bullets Ain't Got No Names" from the days when he was on the field. He rapped in a song that was based on a genuine story, like much of his music, saying, "My hood is warring, so ain't no warnings."

The atmosphere of Puerto Nuevo was entirely different on March 30, 2019. Nip and Firebugg had crossed paths in a public place by chance or fate—Nip with his daughter, Firebug with his fiancée. The stage was prepared for a potent confluence and an unplanned coming together of thoughts.

While Hussle had experienced a remarkable shift from his days of "putting in work" on the set, Firebug had also changed significantly. "Twelve years in prison instilled something in me," he claimed. "Brought me up and awoken me to see the wider perspective as a grown man. Therefore, in hindsight, I can see how beneficial that meeting was. Though he was only passing by for breakfast, as soon as he entered the establishment, Hussle was immediately recognized. He had approached Hussle from behind in order to catch him "slippin '" in the old paradigm. Firebug, though, was no longer feeling that vibe.

"Any type of destructive, any type of violence, anything like that was never on my mind," he claimed. From behind bars, Firebug had been inspired by Nip's success, feeling proud that someone who had endured a similar lifestyle could better himself, start enterprises, and give back to the neighbourhood. I'm looking at a man who hails from the same neighbourhood blocks as me, he remarked. I'm not even talking about the millionaire status; different colour, different side, but transgressed to a level in the game. I'm referring to the neighbourhood humanitarian there. So it was a shock to him when I approached him from behind and saw Nip.

Hussle shared the same enthusiasm. He grinned and said to Firebug, "I'll see you on IG." Genuine nigga shit My niggahs are paying attention, you know. We're not clicking the "like" button. You are aware of what it is. They made the choice to slice it up while seated.

Hussle shook Firebugg's hand and saw a tattoo on his arm as he joined him in the cafe booth. He inquired, "Is that Malcolm?" I've been waiting for you, bro. He had a tight grasp on Firebugg's hand.

Hussle reminded him of their last encounter: "Bro, I got a vision and I been needing a nigga who hold a voice and solid mind state." 2007 took place at the Los Angeles Men's Central Jail. When Hussle got his recording contract, he was on the lam. He celebrated for a week in Jamaica before coming back to L.A. to turn himself in. There was still no release date for the first Bullets Ain't Got No Name mixtape. Tanisha Foster, his girlfriend, was expecting their child, Emani. He had a lot to live for, but on that particular day, everything was in jeopardy.

Hussle remarked, still holding Firebugg's hand, "When I initially fell, I was in the holding tank. The Centinela Park Blood had hazy memories of him. He had experienced so much himself and witnessed a million others inside. Hussle insisted, "Nah. The holding tank contained you. One of your homies had been relocated by one of my homies. He jumped him back because your friend had jumped my homie. When inmates initially arrive for processing, they are all gathered together in the "holding tank," a location where anything can happen, even though criminals in county jail are often separated based on gang affiliation. Fights frequently occur. When battles turn fatal, the body of the deceased prisoner is "packed out." Firebug was beginning to recall. There were more adults than young Crips. They couldn't possibly win. Why did it matter? He exercised his authority to stop the attack at that precise time.

Hussle said, "We came in and you told your homies, 'Nah, we ain't about to jump them. "Bro, I never forgot that."

He never let go of my hand, Firebug said. "And just like that, he took me on a whole journey." They discussed the drive-by shootings that served as the inspiration for the song "Bullets Ain't Got No Names." Hussle recalled telling the man, while on the block with the homies, to "Watch that corner." They could now chuckle about the memories because enough time had gone.

Hussle, who has always favoured action over words, was now acting with greater forethought than ever. He had so many things he wanted to accomplish but so little time. I'm with everything, but I don't have the energy for anything, he declared. Firebug was moved by what he said. The stupid sh*t. the crap act. The shit buster. Snitchin'. They lacked the energy and time to do any of that.

They avoided using the term "peace treaty," as it had already been used. Gang agreements never seem to hold up. Whether the cops broke the cease-fire or someone else did something to someone, the drama usually began again when the pressure built. Another treaty wasn't the answer; ownership and economic empowerment were. Rick Ross and Hussle's "Refinance Version" remix can be thought of as "buying back the block," as they put it in a song. Nip spit, "Operation buy back the 60s," before outside forces could "gentrify the whole inner city, genocide the whole inner city."

Hussle enjoyed walking up to Slauson and passing the shops he and his brother had started, knowing that they had given residents of the area jobs. He was now creating a larger-than-Hyde Park development plan for South Los Angeles. He informed Firebug, "I'm trying to do that all the way to the beach." "But Inglewood is between me and the beach... I've been waiting for someone to speak on your behalf. Who else is going to be able to tell it better than you?

The usually crowded coffee shop was now quiet. Everyone seemed to be angling themselves toward their booth to hear the conversation. Firebugg commented on an Instagram photo of the two of them together, "We both acknowledged the fact we were sworn enemies by gang rights but we declared we were born brothers by essence. Hussle instructed him, "Let's get this flick and fuck the streets up," and he and Emani walked back outside. Afterward, Firebugg's girlfriend remarked, "I felt like I just saw two kings at a sit-down."

After their encounter, Firebug observed, "The word 'peace treaty' will never have to come up when you cross paths with another genuine person. because we already know what game level we are on. A prophet can recognize another prophet when you look deeper than that. He had a chain of Malcolm when he saw him on my arm. I only consider that in retrospect. I didn't realise it until much later.

Soon after his meeting with Firebug, Hussle told Killa Twan about it. Hustle and Nip had been bridging gang lines for years because Hussle's boyhood friend was raised in a Blood neighbourhood. Twan saw the importance of what had happened. These two have engaged in conflict previously, Twan remarked. "They had fired shots at one another before... A horrible situation would arise if it involved another frail person. They were able to sit and talk and eat and converse as men rather than as an Inglewood Blood and a Crenshaw Crip thanks to him being another powerful man like he is.

Angelique Smith had trouble falling asleep. On Sunday, March 31, about 6 a.m., Ermias Asghedom's mother finally fell asleep after struggling to get any sleep till the early morning. She was very spiritual and frequented the KRST Unity Center of AfRaKan Spiritual Science. She lived by the motto, "Everything is in the divine perfect order of our creator." Ermias, Angelique's son, was born on her birthday and she always felt a very close bond with him. She had had a steadfast feeling that something wasn't quite right over the last two weeks.

On the afternoon of Sunday, March 31, Hussle wasn't meant to be at The Marathon Clothing establishment. Although he didn't have a defined schedule, he usually stopped by after dropping Emani off at school on weekday mornings. His bodyguard, J Roc, rarely accompanied him unless there was a public engagement scheduled— especially on a Sunday.

Always by himself, according to Cowboy, a.k.a. Big Thundercat, who collaborated with Hussle on songs and supported Lil Thundercat's hood show in the mid-2000s. He was now a full-time employee of the mall. The only time he ever had serious security was when he was travelling or on tour, according to Cowboy. He "never had security ever" when living in the inner city or travelling to work.

"Nobody's ever at the shop on a Sunday like that," claims DJ V.I.P. Sundays were often reserved for our families and private matters. Because many individuals had girls, kids, and other such things, he thought it was necessary that we always had those days. Nipsey made sure that not only he, but also the rest of us, had time for that.

There were several reasons why this particular Sunday was unique. The previous evening, Hussle had stayed out late to celebrate his godbrother Adam's "C-day" at the stroke of midnight. "Dammy Dam" Andebrhan is credited by their business partner Jorge Peniche as "one of the guys that helped shape a lot of the sonics of the Nipsey Hussle brand and music." Hussle shared a picture on Instagram of him and Adam looking powerful and affluent while wearing white clothes and gold chains. Hussle praised him as "Day 1 with this all $

In Shit! " in the caption. Like Hussle, Adam had grown up with Fatts, and ever since his passing a year and a half earlier, they had both made sure to look after his family.


Nip had travelled to Anaheim on Saturday night before Adam's C-day celebrations to see the Texas Tech Red Raiders defeat Gonzaga Bulldogs and move on to the Final Four of the NCAA Men's Basketball Tournament. Hussle had to make the long trip amid heavy traffic since he couldn't miss this game. Big Bob Francis, an old friend and mentor who gave him the books Contagious, which served as the inspiration for Nipsey Hussle's play Proud2Pay, and The Immutable Laws of Branding, which prodded him to consider himself a brand rather than just an artist, had invited him. Hussle arrived just in time to witness Brandone Francis, the second-string forward for Texas Tech who had boasted to his buddies that his favourite rapper will be in the arena. Francis made a three-pointer as he came off the bench. Brandone's squad won by exactly six points, which was the final score of the game. As loudly as anybody else in the Honda Center, Hussle clapped. He will always be my big brother, Brandone declared. "I'm glad he was there for the historic moment we shared as a team," I said.


Nip's thoughts were buzzing with possibilities after Hussle and Firebugg's unexpected encounter the day before. Since he left the coffee shop, the two had been texting one other. During Centinela's battles with the 1960s, Firebug had lost one of his closest friends. It was a big step for him to put that hurt behind and embrace the idea of oneness.


Hussle was slated to attend a meeting with LAPD commander Michel R. Moore and Los Angeles Police Commissioner Steve Soboroff on Monday, April 1. Soboroff is a rich real estate developer who is also known for creating Staples Center. The Roc Nation letter stated, "Our goal is to collaborate with the department to help enhance communication, relationships, and work toward improving the culture and discourse between LAPD and the inner city. Hussle was a little suspicious after being harassed by the police for so long, but he tried to be open-minded. The cops would either contribute to the problem or the solution, but it was still worth a shot.

That Sunday, as he travelled down Slauson toward The Marathon Clothing flagship shop, he passed the intersection of Crenshaw, where workers were constructing the new light rail line that would quickly transport travellers from LAX to the legendary area where Hussle had set his claim. Nip and Councilmember Marqueece Harris-Dawson collaborated closely to create the Destination Crenshaw idea, which was intended to be a celebration of local culture and a barrier to gentrification.

Local artists, curators, and Zena Howard, a Black architect at Perkins & Will, the firm in charge of creating the Smithsonian National Museum of African American History and Culture, are all involved in the multimillion dollar project. The 1.3-mile "unapologetically Black" open-air museum, which will tell the history of African Americans in Los Angeles, has continued to incorporate Hussle in its preparation. The community art initiative will allow riders of the Metro rail, no matter who they are or where they are going, to become fully immersed in the narrative of Black people in Los Angeles as they pass through the Crenshaw District.

Hussle had these and numerous more ideas as he approached the Marathon store at 2:53 in the afternoon in his black Maybach with All Money In emblems embossed and embroidered all over the interior.

Hussle tweeted something mysterious while waiting in the parking lot: "Having strong enemies is a blessing." He was aware that the majority of his fans would not notice the subtle allusion to Firebug, but as with so much of Hussle's life and work, those that understood would. The actions that will take place during the ensuing 29 minutes could not have been predicted by him. Tick-tick-tick.

"Sam was with Granny at the crib," adds V.I.P., who was in a private meeting in North Carolina at the time. "Nip just stopped by the store to assist the buddy in purchasing some clothing. He had just pulled up to watch out for a neighbour who had just come out when crap happened.

The concerned friend was Kerry Louis Lathan Sr., also known as Cousin Kerry, who was 56 years old. He was born in Houston, migrated to Los Angeles as a youngster, and became a member of the Rollin' 60s. He had served time in prison for a murder conviction in 1996 after being convicted of four prior felonies involving drugs. Being just eleven years old when he was imprisoned, Hussle didn't know Kerry, but soon after Kerry returned home on parole, Nipsey sent him a care box of Marathon gear as a show of support "on hood." Kerry was attempting to rebuild his life, reunite his family, and acclimate to a whole new environment. On that particular day, he claimed he needed some clothing so he could comfort a friend whose children had just lost their father. He explained, "My nephew was whining that because I'm not in jail anymore, I don't have to wear the same outfit. '"You're free.'" Hussle visited The Marathon Clothing store to sign autographs, take photographs with clients, and chat with Cowboy and Rimpau, an old classmate and lifelong musical partner, as he awaited the arrival of Cousin Kerry. Cowboy recounted later, "I was just telling him how proud I was of him. "Just talking and remembering felt like old times again."

At 3:05 p.m., a white Chevy Cruze left Slauson and parked in front of the Master Burger before Kerry arrived. The passenger's visage was one that Hussle was familiar with. He questioned, "Is that Shitty?" Later, when giving evidence before a grand jury, Cowboy stated, "I don't think anybody had seen him in some years." He is a local and one of the homies from the hood.

Hussle's Shitty Cuz, real name Eric Ronald Holder Jr., was a Rollin' 60s member and aspiring rapper who released music under the name Fly Mac. Hussle's estate refuted rumours that he was formerly signed to All Money In, and few people in Hussle's inner circle even remember the man.

Cuzzy Capone claims, "A few people tell me I knew him and I saw him before." Although he might have been in my company, I didn't recognize him. He was obviously not important in my opinion or my life. Just a total nigga and nothing at all. I have no idea who this nigga is.

Gooch claims, "I never heard him rap. But I am aware that he used to hang out in the neighbourhood with some individuals on the street. There were around two or three men rapping over there. I would have heard of him if he were that excellent. People claim that he has visited the studio in the past. Although I don't recall him being there, a lot of individuals have visited the studio while we were writing music or trying to produce but didn't know how to rap. And just because a beat is playing, they decide to start rapping even though no one has said anything to the contrary. And here we are trying to write while you are rapping aloud. It's screwing us all. So I used to tell the security to shut the fuck up, Nigga. Because of that, I've even physically assaulted a few people or simply forced a few to leave.

According to his SoundCloud page, Shitty Cuz wasn't very good or dedicated; over the course of four years, he uploaded just five unimpressive recordings. Nevertheless, Fly Mac added the phrase "plenty niggas hate cuz I'm da great" to his SoundCloud profile in 2015. In person and on his Twitter profile, Hustle had long used the nickname "The Great" to describe himself. But Hussle provided evidence to support his claims of brilliance in the form of captivating lyrics, a unique voice, a sense of flow and melody, charm, integrity, and tenacity—elements that were woefully absent from the few Fly Mac songs that could be heard online. Holder, who was only four years Nip's junior, was unable to match Nipsey Hussle's level of rap industry success.

Holder got out of the car, went into Master Burger to grab some chilli cheese fries, and then strolled over to The Marathon Clothing, where Hussle, Cowboy, and Rimpau were congregating. Holder was showing off his gang tattoos—H60D CRIP at the top of his chest and SIXTIES across his stomach—while shirtless and wearing a black bandanna around his neck.

In Cowboy's recollection of the dialogue, Hussle maintained his composure as Holder drew near. He asked, "Hey, man, what's up." "Where have you been, bro?"

Holder retorted, "I've been out of the way."

Nipsey informed him, "Man, you know they got some documentation on you. You know, I haven't read it. say, you, my brother. Perhaps you should handle that.

In this context, "paperwork" refers to court records that would indicate a person in detention has reached an agreement to lessen their punishment. Those papers, in other terms, would designate him as a "snitch." "Paperwork" is taken very seriously in street culture, where loyalty is paramount and snitching can mean the difference between life and death. It is downloaded, printed, distributed, altered, and discussed in whispers. Messy documentation can have serious consequences, frequently resulting in a "DP," short for disciplinary punishment—a beating, or worse.

The inference was clear: these reports of paperwork were a significant issue that needed to be handled. Neither Holder nor Hussle were heard to reference any particular names or cases as they spoke.

Holder reportedly said, "Oh yeah, motherfuckers be hatin' on me," according to Cowboy.

Do you understand what I'm saying? Nip answered.

Holder said, "No," once more. "People are criticising me,"

At that point, the woman who had driven Holder to the mall exited the Cruze and made her way toward the group of men with the intention of taking a selfie with Nip. The woman's identity has not been made public since she eventually turned informant herself by agreeing to testify against Holder with the Los Angeles County district attorney. In court transcripts, she is referred to as "Witness #1."The driver was granted immunity from prosecution as long as her testimony was entirely accurate under the terms of her agreement with the district attorney. She might still face charges if she was found to have lied while being questioned under oath.

Witness #1 testified under oath that Nip was standing outside as soon as she entered the plaza from Slauson Ave. "Ooh," she exclaimed. "Nipsey Hussle is gone. He seems well. I want to snap a photo. She had heard some of his music and seen him in a BET movie. She continued, "He's cute." "He is attractive." She had been seeing Holder for approximately a month, but he said nothing and made no attempt to show that he was familiar with Hussle.

Witness #1 claims she overheard some of Holden's conversation with Hussle as she walked up for her selfie. She claims that "he was asking Nipsey if Nipsey ever snitched." "Well somebody said," he added, but I couldn't make out the name. Then Nipsey said, "Chill," such as "No, no." Holder repeatedly questioned Witness #1, according to his testimony, "Have you ever snitched? Have you ever come forward?

Witness #1 said, "Nipsey wasn't really talking." "However, his 'no' was simply, 'This person needs to go'... That's how I kind of interpreted it—as an attempt to ignore him. You know how when someone asks you a question repeatedly, you probably don't want to keep answering it? Nipsey was only in that mould. Nipsey then turned to her and announced that he was prepared to snap a photo. Witness No. 1 stated, "I felt honoured." "He didn't reject me at all." As she raised her phone to take the selfie, Hussle leaned against a parked car and wrapped his arm around her. She didn't say anything to Holder before returning to her own vehicle. She uploaded the picture on Facebook to show her pals as soon as she returned to the Chevy Cruze. She said, "I thought it was going to be a dull day, but it turned out fantastic. Everyone was having a good time.

When reading through Witness #1's evidence in the Grand Jury transcripts, she occasionally sounds like a star-struck groupie. Some believe she sometimes comes across as a murder accomplice, such as in the section of her testimony where she discusses the fact that she initially seemed to tell the detectives who were looking into the case that Eric Holder had mentioned wanting to carry out a drive-by, but later seemed to change her story and insist that he had never actually said that. "Why does she have immunity?" you ask. Ralo questioned after talking about the transcripts. He was curious as to why the DA didn't question Witness #1 about a puzzling encounter he had with two individuals by the side of the road just before heading to the shopping centre. Ralo claimed that "he had guns in her car." In order to take a photo with the nigga, the bitch even got out of the car. Do you realise how horrifying that is? When this dude is going to flip, what do you do except jump out and capture his picture? That makes me feel uneasy. And the fact that she has immunity says a lot about how effectively this city combats crime.

The driver provided authorities with a wealth of information given her many interactions with Eric Holder, but Ralo is not the first to cast doubt on her reliability. There were other additional witnesses in the parking lot at the same time who had not yet testified. Another fan, Joshua Baerga, an aspiring actor from New York who goes by the Instagram handle Kid Flashy, was standing close by as Hussle, Holder, Cowboy, and Rimpau were conversing in the parking lot. Kid Flashy chatted to the YouTube vlogger L.A. Show during a three-way phone call while he was being held in custody. (The L.A. Show stands out for doing original reporting, despite the fact that there is a lot of crap about the case on the internet.) Flashy revealed that he had travelled to Los Angeles for a G-Unit Films casting call for a new TV show about the infamous street gang BMF, also known as the Black Mafia Family. After then, according to Flashy, he and a companion went to visit The Marathon Clothing. It appeared to be a contentious discussion, Flashy recalled. Because when I initially approached to attempt to take a picture, I overheard Nipsey telling him, "You can't even be here right now," I kind of retreated because it wasn't the right moment to request images.

Cowboy gave a different account of the conversation's atmosphere. He claimed that there was no indication of hostility. "Had they used any kind of language, I would have led him outside. Had they engaged in any sort of quarrel... In a sense, Nipsey was watching out for him, telling him, "You need to address it," even though I haven't read it and don't know if it's true or not. What Nipsey was doing was that.

Holder's talk with Hussle lasted roughly four minutes and fifteen seconds, according to time codes assembled from multiple security cameras across the retail centre. Cowboy claims that Shitty brought up his music toward the conclusion of their conversation.

Cowboy recalls, "He asked if we heard his rap." 'Yeah, I've been in the studio,' he replied. I performed my newest tune. When he inquired if we had heard it, we responded, "Nah, we haven't heard your song" or something similar. Shitty then turned around and returned to Master Burger.

At 3:08, Holder and Hussle were finishing up their talk when a black SUV driven by his "nephew" Shermi Villanueva came into the plaza parking lot with Cousin Kerry inside. (Family terminology like cousin, uncle, and nephew are also employed to define gang member ties in ways that can be purposefully perplexing.) Kerry gave Hussle a friendly greeting as Holder moved away and then inquired about Cowboy's meal. We were discussing a chicken fajita that is sold at the—what is it? El Pollo Loco, perhaps. It contained chicken and avocados. Since I've been gone for 25 years, I have never seen one.

The Grammy-nominated rapper kept mingling with awestruck customers and signing their merchandise while standing beside parked automobiles in front of The Marathon Clothing door. Kerry stated in an interview that the man had a baby with him when he was shooting the pictures. "His mother requested a photo of herself and her kid. The following day was his third birthday.

When Eric Holder emerged from the Master Burger, he informed Witness #1 that he required two dollars to cover the cost of his meal. He paid for the chilli cheese fries after she gave him a five. He then turned around and headed back toward Hussle.

Cowboy Douglas was testifying before a grand jury on May 6, 2019, when John McKinney, a deputy district attorney, addressed him as he stood on the witness stand. "I want to call your attention now back to the top of the video at the Master Burger door," McKinney said. "It seems Holder returns to your group and walks over again. Observe that? He appears to shake Trump's hand or dap him up, which is another way of saying that he kind of pounds him. He then immediately walks away from the white car while holding something in his hands. Does the video depict that?

"Yes," Cowboy answered.

"Do you remember when that happened?"

"No."

Holder informed Witness #1 that he wanted to consume his food after coming back to the vehicle. She told him, "Not right here," according to her grand jury evidence. He said, "Well, we could just drive around," she claims. After leaving the parking area, she made a right turn onto Slauson.

Holder and Witness #1 left the scene at 3:17, leaving Hussle in the parking lot with Rimpau, Cousin Kerry, Shermi, and a variety of followers while Cowboy entered The Marathon Clothing store to take a lunch break. Kerry claimed he needed the new shirt to visit a friend who was grieving, but he did not accompany Cowboy inside to obtain it.

When Cowboy testified before the grand jury, McKinney, a young Black prosecutor with the L.A. County District Attorney's Office's Major Crimes Division, inquired as to whether there was anything about Holder that made Cowboy wish to separate Nipsey from him. "I felt something in my gut," he admitted. "In that little moment, I thought to myself, Why do I feel this way?... I was already uncomfortable in his presence because of the things he was saying, how he was acting, and how he made me feel.

Cowboy repeatedly referred to Holder's assault as "a straight snake move" on the witness stand and in different on-camera interviews, questioning his own choice to take a lunch break at the precise time he selected. According to him, "I just replay it over and over," he said on the television program Extra. "And I regret that I couldn't have made a different decision. I regret ever leaving his side. You know, there was never any controversy, drama, or conflict. It had no value. It was an outright cunning snake move.

Rimpau did not offer a grand jury testimony and has not spoken in an interview about what happened that day. On April 26, he said on

Instagram, "I beat myself up about MARCH 31st everyday. I wanna do something but ain't nothing I can do to bring you bacc." "I just want to be Shyne with you again." Brodee I worked so hard to get my sh*t together, and I'm delighted you saw my improvement. I appreciate how hard you pushed me and how disciplined you made me. "LLKingNH," or Long live King Nipsey Hussle, was how he signed off on his post.

Witness #1 drove her Cruze around the block after leaving the parking lot, turning right on Crenshaw and then again on Fifty-Eighth Place. The shopping centre and the Shell gas station on the corner are separated by an unmarked lane that they took a second right into. This alley is located between Crenshaw and West Boulevard. Witness #1 claims to have first seen the gun—a black 9mm pistol—at that time. She testified, "I saw him loading the bullets into the magazine while he was pulling out the gun as we were driving... kind of holding it towards the window but not, and I was just like, 'You're not going to do a drive-by in my car.'"

Where did he get the gun, the DA inquired. She remarked, "He pulled it out so quickly I don't know where he got it from." Neither did she notice the semiautomatic handgun when she picked him up shirtless in a neighbouring town earlier that day to go on a 30-minute drive to Los Angeles.

The driver had previously stated that she had seen him carrying a similar rifle during the previous month and that he had claimed he needed it "for protection."

She claimed that he typically wore it tucked under his waistband. Despite the obvious tattoos all over his upper body, she also insisted she was unaware that he was a member of a gang.

Did he mention Nipsey Hussle to you at all? asked DA McKinney. Did he appear to be upset with anyone?

"No," she answered. To me, he appeared to be himself as usual.

"Okay," the DA said, advancing his position. Why did you believe he was going to shoot someone at that precise moment?55

She claimed to have never seen him load a firearm. She said, "Every time he's around me, he simply has it on him. "I never actually saw him installing or fixing anything. I never saw him using it for play. It appears as though he is about to use it.

Witness #1 claims that Holder put the pistol away after she told him she would not put up with any drive-by shooting in her vehicle. She was not pressed further by the DA as to why the notion of a drive-by would even occur to her. She reportedly stated that during her initial interview with police from the Seventy-Seventh Division, Holder requested that she drive him around the block so he could perform a drive-by. Later, she stated that throughout her five-hour interview, the detectives' queries had left her perplexed.

Holder instructed her to halt the car on West Fifty-Eighth Place in the parking area beside the Fatburger restaurant where all of the staff members' clothes are co branded with The Marathon Clothing's signature Crenshaw logo as they completed a second loop of the block. He commanded, "Pull over in here." "I'm hungry." The alley that led to the shopping centre was visible from the front of her car.

He put on a crimson T-shirt while chewing on some chilli cheese fries. Witness 1 claimed to have enquired as to Holder's readiness to go.

Her testimony seemed illogical in some way. Witness #1 was once more pressed by McKinney: Why did you carry a pistol in my car, you didn't ask him? If we're stopped, I might be in trouble for doing this. Anything comparable?

"No," was her response. I simply wasn't considering it... I asked him if he was prepared to leave as I began to drive my car in the direction of the alley. And after that, he said, "Wait. Avoid going nowhere. I'm coming back.

She says she replied, "All right," to him. "Fasten up."

A suspension of disbelief seems to be encouraged in several areas of Witness #1's testimony. Although some of her responses undoubtedly came across as forced, the prosecutor needed her to make the murder case compelling. "Didn't you wonder, 'What is he talking about?'" Asking, McKinney. "'Where is he going?'"

Again, the driver disregarded what seemed like simple, logical solutions. "No," she answered. "I just assumed he might go get something or something," the speaker said. Perhaps he had stuff to buy or forgot something.

"Which way did he turn?"

She claimed that he turned down the alley "towards Slauson way."

Did you ever see him carrying a gun?

"No," she answered. He was merely carrying a takeout container of chilli cheese fries, according to Witness #1. He placed the container on the hood of a white truck that was parked as he made his way toward Slauson through the alley, she claimed. After that, he rounded the street and headed back toward the Master Burger and the parking lot where he had last seen Nipsey.

Hussle was still engaging in fan interaction in front of Marathon while Cousin Kerry had made no headway in obtaining the new shirt that was meant to be the main motivation behind Nipsey's Sunday release.

"Yo, Nipsey man," remarked Kid Flashy to him. "I'm here to participate in 50 Cent's BMF tryout. Would you mind if I took a photo of us and posted it online?

"Yeah, no problem," he replied. I said, "Come on."

Just outside the entrance to The Marathon Clothing, which had a large #CALIFORNIA LOVE hashtag on the plate glass windows in honour of Hustle and Boog's GQ spread, they posed for one last photo. Standing tall in the scorching Los Angeles sun wearing an impeccable white T-shirt, white du-rag, and red shorts with a white drawstring, Nipsey gripped Flashy's hand with a firm grip. He always wore a gold Rolex Presidential, which was on his left wrist.

Kid Flashy started to take pictures when he saw someone coming closer. Flashy remembers, "The kid came back around the corner." "I walked right by him and sensed something wasn't right. I couldn't exactly place it, though. Then I saw him draw away and begin striking him.

When all hell broke free, cousins Kerry and Nipsey were positioned side by side between two parked automobiles. "A guy just came around and started shooting," Kerry said. Kerry testified to the grand jury that the shooter spoke to Hustle just before the rounds were fired. "I believe he said, 'You're through.'"

Kerry was too caught up in the moment to notice the gunman's face. Gunfire was the first thing he reported seeing. "I saw him shoot and that was it, I looked up..." Seeing the flash, You are too close to the gun if you hear gunfire at one o'clock. I then fled.

Holder approached Hussle while fully outstretched in his arms. He held a black semiautomatic in his left hand and a silver revolver in his right hand, both of which could fire at close range. A chunk of Kerry's pelvis bone was chipped off by one of the initial gunshots that struck him in the back just below the belt. It knocked my legs out from beneath me when I turned to run, he claimed. It was warm. hot as fire. He collapsed face-down to the ground. I was moving my feet to check on the functionality of my legs.

Hussle was killed shortly after. Beyond the automobile tire blocking his view, Kerry could make out a portion of his torso laying on the ground. He could hear the shooter's gunfire. He could hear ladies yelling.

DA McKinney enquired as to whether the pattern of firing was continuous or more staccato.

"It was like one, two, three, and then it stopped," Kerry recounted. "And after returning one, two, three more times, it stopped. Then it returned once more. Because I am immobile, I was thinking, "I'm sure this guy is going to finish me off." He didn't, though. Holder fired three bursts of gunfire totaling no less than ten shots.

Kerry overheard Hussle tell Shitty Cuz in three words, "You got me."

Then Shitty approached Hussle and gave him a kick to the head before vanishing.

Cowboy was enjoying his fajita bowl in the Marathon store break area when gunfire suddenly erupted outside. I think I heard a couple gunshots," he claimed. "I started sprinting forward. A few more gunshots were heard. Just as Holder was round the corner and Nipsey was down on the ground, he broke through the front door.

A bullet also struck Shermi Villanueva in addition to Hussle and Kerry. Thankfully, the slug just struck his belt buckle, leaving him dazed but unharmed. Someone yelled to Hussle, "Who did this to you?" He mentioned a name, but Kerry was unable to make it out.

Witness #1 was using her phone to check social media while the car's engine was running when she heard the gunfire. Although she was parked so she couldn't see the plaza, she did spot a man racing in that direction. "I was just like, 'Oh my God,'" she recalled. "'What's happening? Wishing you well. You must move quickly. The first thing she thought was, "Let me get out of here." She didn't, though. "I didn't know if he got hurt or something happened," she admitted in court. So I attended to him.

District Attorney McKinney posed a straightforward inquiry. "Did it ever occur to you that he might have fired the gunshots you heard?" She once more replied "no."

Later, Holder could be seen sprinting up the alley. She questioned as soon as he got in the car, "What's going on?" "Drive," he commanded. Before I slap you, drive. Never before had he addressed her in such a manner. She demanded, "What's going on?" He responded, "You talk too much."

"I just kept driving," said Witness #1. I didn't want him to strike me or do anything similar.

Even though LAPD investigators' download of security camera footage showed Holder with a revolver in each hand, the driver claims she didn't see anything until after he got into the car. She remarked, "He had the revolver on this side of him. It was as though he didn't want me to see it. The bag that his chilli cheese fries had been delivered in was where he hid the handgun. The DA questioned, "You knew something bad had happened in that parking lot at that point, didn't you?" What occurred, in your opinion, in the plaza parking lot? She remarked, "I just felt like I knew there was shooting going on. I was unsure as to whether he was the shooter. I was unsure whether he was being shot at. I only knew that something had occurred.

When the phone rang at Granny's house, Sam answered it. "He got the call and he ran out of here so fast," Margaret Boutte remarked. He never acts in such a way. She took up the phone and called her daughter as soon as he departed. She said, "Angel, something must have happened." Sammiel stood up. He skipped his shower. He left this place so quickly. Sam pushed the gas pedal all the way to Crenshaw, speeding down Slauson while dodging red lights.

Cowboy stated, "I rushed over to Nip and grabbed him. He was cognizant in and out, but he had a pulse. But he struggled mightily. His T-shirt had crimson stains on it. To stop the bleeding, the cowboy applied pressure with his hands. According to Cowboy, "He was still breathing and biting a little bit of his tongue." "If his eyes began to droop slightly, I yelled, "Nip, wake up!" And he would quickly recover. Cowboy had little choice but to pray and wait for the paramedics.

Blacc Sam arrived first. He had been concerned about his younger brother experiencing anything similar for a long time. He thought to himself, "There's no reason for him to still be alive," observing bullet wounds in Nipsey's left leg, stomach, and underarm. Sam focused intently on the 911 operator while counting chest compressions and attempting to tune out the commotion around him.

Sam would subsequently tell the Los Angeles Times that "Nip is sporadic." "Nip is going to pull up and jump out of the Jordan Downs projects, Nickerson Gardens, or any other neighbourhood in Los Angeles, Compton, or Watts—alone with $150,000 in jewellery on his neck and a $80,000 Rolex without security. Because of this, the populace adored him.

Sam let the paramedics take over when they eventually arrived. In an effort to calm Hussle down, the EMS crew gave him an IV and a breathing tube. When they moved him onto a stretcher, they discovered the head wound.

When Killa Twan initially learned Nip had been shot, he kept his composure. A half-hour prior, he had just finished speaking with Hussle on the phone. Twan had just missed him because he was at The Marathon Clothing picking up shirts and socks. We've gone through a lot, he reminded himself. 'He's fine,' I said.

Then someone pointed out an Instagram Live post to him and said, "Nah, bro, you need to go check." He hurried from Watts to Crenshaw, getting there just as his friend was being taken to the hospital. The neighbouring cousin of Twan grabbed him and said, "Bro, you don't wanna see."

He replied with astonishment, "Huh?" But he's going to be alright, right?

His cousin silently shook his head. "Nah, brother, go."

Are you certain? Twan enquired.

He heard his cousin say, "Man, we know. "We've seen that garbage much too often. We have witnessed far too many dead bodies. Screw what they're talking about. He has already left.

Twan saw the paramedics removing Nipsey from the scene. "I remember the white turban he had on his head," he relates. "I noticed how red it was as they were loading him into the ambulance. I responded, "Hell nah."

When Angelique Smith arrived at the shopping centre, her son had already been carried away by paramedics. She questioned a policeman who was on the scene, "What happened?"

The cop answered, "Someone was shot."

She questioned, "Who?"

Mr. "Nipsey Hussle."

"Oh, oh, my soul said. I'm done now. During a memorial event at the BET Awards, she recalled "that's why." I had finished thinking about my son's murder. Her choice of words—assassination rather than death or murder—was noteworthy.

Soon after the guns rang out, Rimpau fled the area and later returned to the retail centre appearing disturbed. She attempted to touch the buddy of her son by placing her hands on his shoulders. "Look into my eyes, Evan," she said. You are aware, Evan, that we are spiritual beings enjoying a physical existence. You do realise that, right? As a result, even when our bodies "die" on this side of eternal, our spirits continue to exist. We ascend from this ship and carry on. She sensed a spirit of vengeance and retaliation encircling him. She remembered, "I don't even know what words I used because I was so scared then. She believed, however, that she had ultimately "chased those spirits away from him."

At DJ Mustard's place, YG was observing March Madness on television. Duke and Michigan State were competing for the opportunity to take on Texas Tech in the Final Four. Ty Dolla $ign and YG placed a wager on the contest. He received a call from Jade, his "day-one homegirl" who worked at the Marathon shop, informing him that Nipsey had been shot. She called back just as YG was bringing Mustard the news to confirm that he had been shot four times. When told which hospital he was being transferred to, YG got into his truck and inquired.


Then she called back and said something different. I simply rose and walked away. I walked over to my truck. I got in the truck and started driving away. 'Where y'all going,' I ask. Where are you going, bro? I then drove by Mustard's house, and he was already in the car. "Shit, I thought you left already," he said. "Nah, hop in my shit," I say. We all then got into my truck. They also told us where they were taking our brother. And indeed, we were around fifteen to twenty minutes away as we travelled. 'Homie ain't gonna make it,' they say.

# CHAPTER 8

# HIGHER AND HIGHER

Hussle's preferred barber and braider was Seattle-based Tatum Herman. He would often say, "She's the truth." Whenever she was available, he would bring her along on tour even though she didn't much like travelling.

Nipsey was a little apprehensive when Herman was requested to braid her hair for the wake. I brought his favourite tea, she recounted, "so the whole room would smell good. I brought some crystals, sage, and palo santo with me. I had to be at a specific location, so it was a ritual. Though it would be more difficult that day, she could feel his presence.

She claimed that Nip "was very tender-headed." He would be moving around, and he couldn't manage it, I mean. I heard him say, "T, this is the first time it didn't hurt," as I was doing the first braid, and I swear to God I heard him. I was there with his spirit.

Hussle's presence was felt by many people that day, not just Herman. Kameron Carter, Lauren's nine-year-old son, addressed the crowded Staples Center audience. He stated, "I had a dream on the night of April second. "Ermias suddenly materialised behind me as I was enjoying myself in paradise's ocean. What's up, Killa? he exclaimed.That's my nickname for him, after all. I yelled his name, turned around, and hugged him. He quickly left, but I suppose it was still cool.

Kameron recalls telling his mother about the dream while sporting a tie and blazer with an image of Hustle on the lapel. "I was reflecting after I told her what I had said when I remembered that Ermias had described what heaven was like to me. It was wonderful, he assured me.

Kameron recalled his stepfather greeting him each day with "Respect" as he stood at the window in the morning. He instructed the audience, "So on the count of three I want everyone to yell RESPECT," before starting the countdown. Three, two, and one. Upon his order, 21,000 voices joined together to form one. "Respect!"

Kameron concluded, "In honour of Ermias Asghedom." August 15, 1985, to March 31, 2019.

At the memorial service, Killa Twan claims to have been in the front row. Epic, I tell you. Amazing, I must say. I shall never forget that; it was something. I didn't believe it would be that way, despite how frequently he mentioned selling out the Staples Center. That crap had already sold out.

Wack 100, the manager of Blueface and The Game, said in a contentious No Jumper interview months later, "He packed out Staples Center at a funeral." But have you seen Nipsey Hussle perform at the Staples Center, where his loyal fans turned out in droves to support him? Three nights in a row, I saw Kendrick Lamar perform to packed houses. Just stats here, folks. No personal opinions are being discussed. Hussle's career had not yet reached that point when he passed away, in Wack's view, making him ineligible for "legend" designation. Is what happened messed up? Wack spoken. "What happened was definitely screwed up. Do I wish we could turn back time so he could do it all over again? Definitely. Was there a loss for hip hop? Definitely." Hussle did not, in Wack's opinion, merit the title of legend. Because of the lack of support from his followers, the media, and other factors, we did not lose a legend at the time. Will he arrive there in the end? I think it is. Was he, as they claim, that person when he died? Undoubtedly not. And all we're doing is talking about statistics. Wack was later hit in the face backstage at Rolling Loud by Hussle's security J Roc, who didn't like what Wack had to say.

At the Staples Center, others including Smoke DZA and Jonny Shipes paid their respects. His service was very difficult to describe, according to DZA. Not even a routine service was provided. Each of us was in mourning. The NBA Finals were being watched, and it was a show. Regarding the individuals present, it was everything. He's probably giggling over some shit, I'm sure of it. Kendrick Lamar and LeBron James are also available. It was a who's who list. Inside the Staples Center, he was honoured by all of these folks. DZA laughed when he claimed that Michael Jackson was the only other person to have had a funeral in the Staples Center. Can you feel me? That's the level at which my man was operating.

Blacc Sam, like his brother, has always preferred demonstration to speech. He wasn't one for lengthy speeches, but during his brother's memorial, the words flowed beautifully. Sam talked about how he and his brother had modelled themselves after the optimistic people, the hustlers, while standing up at the Staples Center on live television. He remarked, "They didn't even have to say anything to us. "They demonstrated through deeds. And you are aware that was the theme of Nip. Demonstrating before returning to allow visitors to approach, touch, and observe.

His brother claimed that the encouraging remarks were the ones that Nip valued. Sam remarked, "The pats on the back, it meant a lot to him, whether he expressed it or not. Keep doing what you're doing, bro. "We value what you're doing," You're putting us on the map, and you're making it look good. He valued that garbage highly. The fact that everyone did that meant a lot to me.

Sam referred to a line from Hussle's song "I Don't Stress," saying, "If I die today I made the set proud, nigga." Sam spoke to his brother while struggling to contain his emotions as the Staples Center erupted into a loud ovation. You made the entire globe happy! You realise? Bro, look at this garbage.

Without a question, Hussle's legacy has inspired pride throughout the world. His visage is now recognizable all over the world because of the murals that depict him across the city. Book clubs were started in Hussle's honour to read and debate his favourite novels because of his love of literature and the reading lists he would share with pals.

Sam continued after taking a time to collect himself. "A lot of people believed that when he originally signed, he would make some money and then depart. They had absolutely no idea, as he had previously stated. They had no idea what he was actually going to do. Everyone should be aware, Nip. Sam took an extended pause, focusing "his heart and soul on Crenshaw and Slauson."

As brothers go, Samiel and Ermias Asghedom were extremely close. They discussed everything, including death, with one another. Sam responded, "We used to talk." "We must leave. We are unsure of when we will depart—at 80, 60, 30, or 20. But the most important thing is to make sure you travel the proper route. You defend what you hold dear. You back up what you say with deeds. You never give up. Never allow peer pressure stop you from following your passion. Never let politics or anything else keep you from becoming involved and sticking around. I hope everyone is aware that's what my brother did. On Crenshaw and Slauson, Bro remained and passed away. Nip had nothing but love for everyone who displayed love, including those who did not. There is nothing but love, respect, and humility.

Hussle requested that a Stevie Wonder song be played at his funeral in the song "Ocean Views," which he wrote. On April 11, 2019, Wonder performed live at the Staples Center. But he needed to say something first. The R&B legend claimed, "I knew him from hearing his music. I also had the pleasure through someone who's extremely close to my wife—Pastor P—who arranged a meeting for me to have a meeting with him so that we could converse. I had the opportunity to meet both Lauren and him. The occasion was Pastor P's birthday. but also acknowledging that we had a fantastic discussion and anticipated a happy life.

To lose a family member once more is heartbreaking, Stevie continued. "Because it's so pointless, it breaks my heart. Even though we claim to be a civilised society and a world, we continue to live in a time when ego, rage, and jealousy rule our daily activities. Knowing that there aren't enough individuals speaking out in favour of stricter gun control measures is really upsetting. Though too late to save Hussle, the Staples Center applauded his statements. Even so, they applauded.

There were still more tales to be shared and more tears to be shed even after Stevie's final song was performed. The faithful left the Staples Center in a line and were met by the late-afternoon sun. Tens of thousands of mourners crowded Los Angeles' streets, riding horses, motorbikes, ATVs, and youngsters on their moms' shoulders. They clambered on roofs and climbed lampposts to get a better look of the L.A. royalty as he passed past. Overhead, helicopters were hovering. Marching bands played with enthusiasm, and from every angle, Nip Hussle the Great's voice could be heard reverberating over his realm. White gloves were worn by Hussle's pallbearers as they carried his body into a silver hearse with an Eritrean flag on the roof and drove him through his city's neighbourhoods one more time. As his procession drove through the streets of Los Angeles, backed by motorcyclists and adoring crowds all along the 25-mile route, well-wishers turned out to pay their respects wherever they passed.

I don't care what it was—it was Bloods, Crips, Hispanic, or Asian, remarked Cowboy. "The whole city expressed affection in every hood we rolled through. We travelled from Slauson and Crenshaw all the way to Watts by rolling.

Steve Lobel remarked, "I want to salute the L.A. police." "They didn't come in forcibly and demand people to leave and this and that during the parade and everything at his shop and everything. They recoiled and released it. I've witnessed instances where riots break out when the police get overly protective or order people to leave. And just to see the helicopters, drones, and other equipment was fantastic. He was walking through all the enemy hoods, and it was insane, and they were just enjoying him. He overcame several obstacles. God may have therefore needed him.

When the memorial service was held, Dexter Browne was in Trinidad with his family, grieving the loss of the charismatic, complex son he had raised. We losing him truly upset us, he remarked. It truly affected us negatively. Given our experience, it was painful not to be able to attend the funeral. Dexter was reminded of all the funerals that Hussle had paid for by the elaborate memorial. "His allegiance to the hood never wavered," recalls Dexter. "When he got on and started making money, he didn't." "He would pay for the funerals for the homies who got shot and stuff like that, and it obviously would give him some power over time. He succeeded in becoming what he desired. Although I don't believe he intended to sacrifice his life for it, sometimes your dreams don't come true precisely how you want them to.

Following the ceremony, Jorge Peniche was contacted by Atlantic Records to create billboards in Hussle's memory. They urged him to act because "the city and the people are hurting like they lost a family member," they said. Hussle's real family was devastated, even if the city was in pain. Peniche claimed that those who knew him well were "completely devastated, broken into a million pieces." He believed the picture would aid in the healing process. With the goal of "reviving the spirit of resilience and also celebrating the legacy, greatness, and legend of Nip Hussle," he got to work.

Peniche remarked, "We had to do it. "We had to display a billboard depicting that." On the day his wife, the television personality Letty

Peniche, gave birth to the couple's second son, the design was completed. Peniche said, "We were in the delivery room." "My wife had just arrived. We had only begun to settle in. We were just attempting to find out how to create it, and my photo was the only creative element.

The photo was taken by Roc Nation executive Lenny S on the set of the "Higher" music video. Sam used the word "Prolific," which at this point was considered to be synonymous with Nipsey's name, Peniche recalled. "Something he claimed ownership of and had permission to use. I then replied, "Okay, Prolific." This is fantastic. He was still in mourning as he sat in the delivery room with his laptop, awaiting the arrival of his kid.

He told himself, "I really have to dig deep and find inspiration to do this." I give Nip credit, man," he remarked. "I believe he helped guide it, and I had my antenna up. Just as he would with any previous action we've taken. Much of it was inspired by his brilliance. And then it says, "Okay, I know how to do it." How about we try this? else "How about we do that?" Therefore, I believe that set of billboards was not an exception. The term "prolific," which Hussle had tattooed on his face, was written out by the man. a term Hussle used in the first line of the song "Victory Lap" to identify himself. From one side of the billboard to the other, he wrote the word in capital letters using Franklin Gothic, the emblematic font of Marathon. It felt really appropriate, he said. "And I made the photo as large as I could. Nips were placed, snuggled between letters, and I trimmed as precisely as I could around him in Photoshop. The design took fifteen minutes to complete. His mother-in-law then approached him and informed him that his son was soon to be born after he had sent the document to the team. They gave the child the name Luis Ermias Peniche in tribute to Hussle.

"I'm a man of faith, and I believe that Nipsey's spirit lives with us," the pleased father declared. And I can see all the different ways he's manipulating things. Boy, man—this guy is doing some amazing things for his team and the individuals he cares about. His influence will last forever.

The billboards are seen by Peniche as a gift for the city. People are both getting better and hurting, he added. "Nipsey represented more than just a fantastic artist; he also served as a source of inspiration and an example that... "I can do it too."

After Nipsey was killed, Ralo states, "I feel like the love is gone from over here." "I realize I'm probably biased since that's my nigga, but over here, it's never going to be the same. There is a gap. It appears that both the love and the lights have vanished.

Ralo claims that after Hussle was killed, a level of rage overcame him that he had never felt before. It appeared as though the room would become silent and still, he claims. "I could have killed and then immediately eaten a meal. If I hadn't brought it up, it would never have happened. I had to ask God to take the heat off of me. I was enraged like a demon, he continued with a grimace.

Ralo was fortunately able to leave the city, spend some time in Atlanta, and gather his thoughts. He gave his decisions as a teenager—both his own and Ermias'—a lot of thought. "It made me realise what was missing when I came off the porch," he claims. "I didn't feel like that during my teens, therefore that was the cause. I find it hard to imagine feeling that way at the age of thirteen. Think about your friend being killed. You cannot go away. Simply stroll by the area where your friend's blood was spotted on the sidewalk. You need to keep checking behind you, even though you're not sure why. It initiates such a strong sense of hatred that it is impossible to expunge. You won't be the same again. Your physical self will changThe coronavirus has caused a delay in the murder trial for Eric Holder. He was hauled into court for a preliminary hearing in July 2020 while being bound at the wrist and knees and wearing chains around his waist. His yellow top and blue jumper pants suggested that he was in isolation and being detained in an area known as High

Power, where high-profile offenders are kept apart from General Population, according to Alex Alonso, a gang expert and professor at California State University Long Beach. Holder was accompanied by defence lawyer Lowynn Young, who has been defending him ever since O.J. Simpson's famous lawyer Christopher Darden withdrew from this case owing to threats to his life. Eric Holder is the target of a lot of anger. On the internet, there are unconfirmed allegations about the deaths or suicides of several members of his family, including his father, as well as other conspiracy theories. Holder's attorney explained to Judge Robert Perry during the hearing that she had been unable to prepare a defence because she required specific information from discovery but was unable to reach D.A. McKinney, who was absent from court that day.

Holder, who was detained outside a mental facility, might never be put on trial. He might negotiate with the prosecution or enter an insanity plea. The death of Nipsey Hussle will undoubtedly join those of Malcolm X, JFK, Biggie, and Tupac on the list of unsolved mysteries, despite the fact that the case has officially been solved. There are numerous ideas circulating online, ranging from pharmaceutical firms to an Illuminati sacrifice.

One LAPD cop who requested anonymity so that he could speak freely said, "I've heard all of the conspiracy theories." "I just say keep it simple," you know, the Muslim women and the new mothers. Similar to how Tupac leapt on a man, who then moved closer and shot the man. But other individuals want to portray it as being the FBI and other such things. However, the detective thinks that someone had to authorise the murder during the Rolling 60s. "In gangs, you do have to have the okay to pull the trigger," he claims. "You can't shoot someone like that without also risking consequences for you and your family. I'm aware of that. Sometimes you have to get permission. Hey, man, I'm going to do that. After that, take care of your business or whatever. Asking Ralo what happened to Nip is not worthwhile. "I'm not willing to lose my life to answer that question," he declares. Like Cuzzy and many of Nipsey

Hussle's closest friends, he rejects the claim that Hussle was killed at random because of a quarrel with another cast member.

Cuzzy claims, "It just seemed like it's more than a fluke." Since I honestly don't know what happened, I won't say that he was set up to it. My mind is constantly thinking. What I will say is that this wasn't a coincidence at all, man. I think there was a lot of planning behind that thing."

"It's just street shit," declares Killa Twan. It's not any of the additional nonsense that the administration is trying to pass off as truth. It's the fight we all face on a daily basis here in Los Angeles. Being a young Black man simply wanting to make a difference and show others another way. Regardless of what you do, someone will despise you. That's the sad thing, though. Twan claims that prior to the day of the murder, he had never heard of Shitty Cuz. "It's not a topic worth discussing. People in the inner circle are aware of what is going on and how it will be handled. That's the stuff it is. Nothing like the tired, "Oh, the government, Dr. Sebi..." No. Real street stuff, that.

Ralo claims that "anyone who looks like a savior in the Black community is gunned the fuck down." "It's a story... Like, we already know how the movie will finish. And it's awful that we can all agree that's not what happened because we want things to return to normal. I've grown to detest us. In the 1970s, we wouldn't have chosen this. In the 1990s, we wouldn't have taken the risk.

There is no doubt that Nipsey Hussle's death was not in vain. His influence is seen everywhere. His image has joined that of Malcolm X and Tupac as a symbol of emancipation. Ralo ponders Nipsey's potential viewpoints on the 2020 national uprising and calls for racial reckoning. He says, "I long to know what he would be doing now— him and Kobe. "Two of our city's most inspiring citizens. Those two individuals. Do you remember how it felt to be around people who weren't Black at the time? Everyone was looking down. It seemed like we were constantly losing our wind. Then came the Coronavirus. We are unable to even breathe.

Ralo claims that the Smithsonian will eventually house Hussle's chains. He was so shocked by the news that he started giggling. Ralo comments, "That's the second thing my homie did to impress me from beyond the grave." The first occurred on the day of the memorial when he cast a cloud in the form of his face over Crenshaw and Slauson. Everyone saw it, according to Ralo. Everyone posted it online. It was outstanding. I would never walk with a man and develop a fervent devotion to him after he passed away. We hadn't entirely made up our differences. But it's simply so extraordinary that the entire tale must be conveyed from that level of mystique," he chuckles. "I'm popping this shit, so there's like glittering dust, like fairy dust, in the room right now."

He is astounded that Hussle "planned past his flesh" and maintained his agenda. "That's heavy duty business," Ralo remarks. The phrase "leaving a legacy" is frequently used, but in order to truly achieve it, one must speak from beyond the grave. And the only way you could accomplish it while you were here was if you were totally focused. He sketched out this stuff. People like Ralo are motivated by this example to ensure that The Marathon is maintained. He says, "We've got to carry the torch." It's no longer even a marathon. Relay, that is. Numerous others received the baton from Nipsey, without a doubt. He gave a lot of people authority.

Just before the 2020 election, Samantha Smith stated through Instagram Live, "Yes, they are afraid of what we can do. "And they want us to always live below our means. It's how they triumph. By forcing us to remain under the lowest degree of control, they are able to maintain their control and power. So people, climb and don't be afraid. Speaking the truth will result in a lot of backlash. Lead the way. Don't follow others. Do not let the opinions of those around you deter you from acting on your own convictions. Do it now. Vote only, please. Who has something to lose? One method to keep the

Marathon going is through increasing public knowledge of important topics and assisting in the voting process. Sales of "FDT," her brother and YG's song that serves as a protest song, increased by 1,200% the week before the election. The song, which received one million streams on election day, encouraged record-breaking voting turnout, especially among Black Americans, who ultimately ousted Trump.

The final song Hussle ever released, "Racks in the Middle," featuring Roddy Ricch and Hit-Boy, received two Grammy Award nominations after his passing. Due to a 2,776 percent increase in music sales after his death, it has now become his highest-charting song and peaked at number 44 on the Billboard Hot 100. However, portions of the lyrics have changed as a result. That music isn't something I listen to, Jonny Shipes says. "It makes my heart ache."

Hussle laments the passing of his boyhood friend Fatts in the song's second stanza. In the music video for the song, Nipsey pays a visit to his friend's grave. He raps, "Damn, I wish my nigga Fatts was here. How did you pass away at thirty or so after having smoked for so many years?

Hussle freely acknowledged crying while recording that verse in the studio.30 The top of the second stanza of the song, where Hussle sings, "Under no condition would you ever catch me slippin'," is just as cruel as what he says about Fatts. If only that were the case, but the reality is that individuals can't always be on high alert, especially in their familiar surroundings.

"I wish I woulda been there," the original Slauson Boy Hoodsta adds. Rob. Because it was different for my brother and I. You realise? I was a member of the group, but I also kept an eye on him. G Bob kept an eye on him as well. Everything, including the musical component, was wonderful. But I was aware that I had a duty to watch over my brother. So I was never distracted from watching him because I was too engrossed in what was happening. I would jump in front of the gun if I were there. But every event has a purpose. They are aware of the fact that it was my brother. You must be aware of your place in a greater whole.

"There's a certain air of 'Oh, but I'm here,'" Ralo explains. And when you feel that way, you'll let down your guard. You eventually arrive there. So whatever that means, that means. After you settle in, you are rocked to sleep.

In an interview with the lyrics website Genius, Hussle remarked, "We always were aware of playing defence, and protecting ourselves." However, I now have three complete gun cases, so I no longer play that way. I'm not here toying around with my daughter's safety like that. If I go to jail, everything will halt. Additionally, hiring the shooter is less expensive than posting bail. We simply had to start thinking in terms of levels because even if you win the case, the bail is more expensive than your paycheck.

Nipsey, his elder brother, and their business partner had just paid $2.5 million for the shopping centre where their store was located, but on March 31, 2019, they arrived without security. The gunman was able to fire on Hussle, run away, fire again, retreat once more, and then return a third time to fire the final shots before fleeing from what should have been a suicidal attempt, as evidenced by the video surveillance.

"That shit hurt me the most," admits Rick Ross, who worked with Hussle on classic recordings and attempted to persuade him to sign with Maybach Music Group. "Homie was outside wearing basketball shorts and a white T-shirt. That is similar to being at home. When it happens, you're at your most relaxed. Because he could have easily had fifteen men in all black, each armed with a machine gun, waiting there with just one phone call, I'm sure. The last time I was with him, the sun was setting, and he seemed so content and at home. I began to wonder whether it was time for me to leave before I brought any unwanted energy.

Ross is completely aware of the challenges involved in transitioning from a local hero to a well-known national rapper. It's not a secret when I relocate to specific locations, he claims. "I'm going to set up a few things. I want to feel just as relaxed in my basketball shorts as he did. And I've experienced those similar suicide attempts. not once, not twice, and possibly even more times than I could count. However, before you stop returning home, you say, "Fuck it." As regrettable as that may sound, you have to do what you have to do. I continue to drive the foreign vehicles through my area because I consider it to be part of my profession. Because that is how I was motivated, that is how I encourage the young people.

"For him to lose his life in the place he gave so much to, it's a life lesson for everyone," says Master P, a New Orleans music tycoon whose No Limit empire rewrote the rules for independent rap companies and served as an inspiration for Nipsey Hussle's All Money In movement, among other things. "There are demons out there, so you still have to be able to understand the environment you're in."

P was in the studio with Hussle two days before his death, working on the song "Street Millionaire" for the I Got the Hook-Up 2 soundtrack. P recalls, "His mind was happy." He recently constructed a studio and wanted everyone to see it. I did it, man, he exclaimed. I recently purchased this building over here, I run a business, and I just closed a transaction on some shoes. He is moving forward. He had a wonderful connection with his girlfriend. He was a father. Everything was in his favour. He was, in my opinion, at his happiest. He had no hatred for anyone. When I called him, he would respond, "What you need, big dog?" Nobody could have predicted this. The devil just showed up.

Meek Mill started with Charlamagne Tha God, "Me and Nipsey got different thinking frames. "I believe that while we had two quite distinct mental frameworks, we were similar in certain aspects. Me, you ain't never see me back in the hood without a gun around, close—and I'm talking about in a legal way," the Philadelphia rapper stated. The rapper wears a chain in memory of Hussle and Lil Snupe, a musician who was killed in 2013 and was a member of Meek's Dreamchasers record label. No young kings should be shot and killed in the neighbourhood. Just for that, he is legendary. You managed to escape, but a jerk shot and killed you. You are a legend; you proved to young people that it is possible to succeed; yet, someone from your own country will drag you back and kill you. I can assure you that Nipsey likely had an impact on hundreds of millions of slum youngsters. They are fully aware that if they try to live out their dreams of remaining in the ghetto, their lives will be taken from them. Just that message in isolation.

Even though Cuzzy Capone has been deeply affected by the passing of his friend, he isn't ready to give up on the hood. "You've got to really handpick who you're fucking with, and make sure they're in control of their own life," he advises. "Make sure nothing is actually following them because that shit... You know where it goes. You may see what took place in my brother's life. We have never been the city where these producers and labels are eager to meet up with us and have a fling or grab a nigga. Everywhere is wild-ass shit, but there's something uncool about Los Angeles. You understand what I mean? Biggie was killed by Niggas. Here, Biggie passed away. Pac was slain by Niggas. Nip was slain by Nigas. This entire thing has its roots in L.A. niggas. It's astounding, buddy, the level of hatred and evil on the streets out here.

In the days after Hussle's death, tributes would take place in towns all around the world. Rapper Dave East from Harlem, who worked with Nipsey Hussle on songs including "Clarity" alongside Bino Rideaux, staged a candlelight vigil in New York City on Monday, April 1. Dave East wiped away emotions as he paid tribute to Hussle while holding a Mylar N balloon in his hand and a blue cloth over his head. "A sucka took out a fuckin' king," he declared. "A true ruler for the time. I couldn't sense that because I was a child during Pac and Big. This feeling is horrible. Candles in hand, a mob of mourning shouted, "Facts! Facts! Facts!" I'm not no revolutionary nigga, Dave

East continued. I don't give sermons. I don't even do this. I'm fuckin' used to shows. This is not what I do. It's my brother there. You can smell me? I'm going to do this if no one else in New York City does it first.

One of the many notables who pay respect to Hussle on Instagram was Nas, the renowned MC who signed East to Mass Appeal Records and was admired by Hussle. We are in a terrible situation right now, he wrote. This is painful. Direct and to the point. Being an MC can be risky. Being a basketball player is risky. Having money puts you in danger. To Be A Black Man Is Dangerous. So much animosity. We have a lifestyle similar to that of our relatives in developing nations. America has it right. We should base our decisions regarding our own lives on the possibility that we won't survive. It's firmly entrenched. It's difficult to correct. When children are still enduring poverty, fixing anything is difficult. I won't stop talking, though. Nipsey is a voice for real. He cannot be kept from speaking. He is still an honourable general who has never abandoned his people.

According to Blacc Sam, "all the memorial services all over the world are just a testament to how many people he touched." "It's a monument to his message, to what he stood for, and to the many lives he touched and inspired. He really was the champion of the people. The narrative is merely creating something out of nothing. Additionally, he was inspirational and never believed himself to be superior to anyone. Simply continuing to do so will demonstrate to others that anything is possible if you have faith and persevere. Everyone in every neighbourhood and region of the country admired, respected, and revered Nip for that. It's moving to see them express their affection.

His younger sister, Samantha Smith, told me, "I feel like it's beautiful that so many people have been able to connect with such a special, chosen person." "It just serves to affirm who he is as a person. I'm just happy that the entire world is aware of him because I already knew he was this kind of person. The chief technology officer of All Money In, Iddris Sandu, takes up the torch and tries to find some silver lining in this humbling setback. He remarks, "I find it really fascinating how everything is finally coming full circle." "I don't think this is a tragedy, which is why I use the word intriguing instead of tragic. Actually, it's a breakthrough. Saying it is tragic would suggest that his message won't be carried on. It's a breakthrough because so many people—whether they knew Nipsey or not—who were affected by him are now coming forward to express their support. To me, it represents a breakthrough.

Could the passing of such a remarkable person be seen as a breakthrough in some way? Maybe—in a way. Samantha, though, is unable to ignore the devastating loss. She added, "It also upsets me because at the end of the day I feel like the world lost such a significant person too. I feel like I lost such a significant person in my personal life, in our family.

Gary Vaynerchuk, a businessman and pioneer of social media, recalls how easily he and Nipsey clicked because they had a love for what Hussle called "creative destruction, the risky business of going against the grain." Gary Vee realised that Hussle and he both thought in terms of fifty years even though they hailed from quite different cultures. When this incident occurred, "he wasn't as big in the macro as Pac and Biggie," claimed Vaynerchuk. "However, many individuals who had never heard of him exclaimed, 'Whoa! Why are the biggest names in the game still writing so emotionally?' He had an effect on you right away if you had the privilege of even getting to know him a little.

"The meaning of Nip Hussle has taken on universal resonance and meaning now," said David Gross, the L.A.-born real estate investor and developer who supported the Asghedom brothers' purchase of the plaza at Crenshaw and Slauson, giving them a foundation from which to uplift themselves and their neighbourhood. "People understand who he was everywhere,"

His "Our Opportunity" project was created to give those who cared about the welfare of the people in the neighbourhoods in which they were investing access to the power of Opportunity Zones. Gross had not given up on their objectives a year after Hussle's passing, but his perspective had grown more expansive. He told Van Lathan at Vector90, "I do want to get Tip, and I do want to get 2 Chainz and Meek and [Allen Iverson]," during their conversation. I want to gather everyone who is a local hero, and together, let's go purchase up their city since they have capital gains. However, it would not be faithful to my original notion that Nip and I always had to work in tandem with the community.

In order for inhabitants of the 8,700 designated regions to obtain tax advantages for investing in their own communities, Gross says he would want to see the Opportunity Zone Act changed; however, in the meantime, he is using the instruments at his disposal. Gross started the Investor Challenge through Our Opportunity with the goal of "awakening people who have never invested before," and offered to seed new accounts with $100 grants. One of the first to get in touch and give support was Trae the Truth, a rapper and activist from Houston who was close to Nipsey Hussle. Since then, other people have adopted the concept, which is still spreading across the nation. On the ground floor of Vector90, Gross is instructing core economics and finance courses. Another program called Own Our Own enables locals to contribute $1,000 to a real estate investment fund.

According to Gross, "I'm putting into those deals the same diligence I'd put into something me and Nip would do." In order to preserve the culture and prevent eviction, the ultimate objective is to "harness as much money that is community-aligned, that's in the hands of individuals who care, who originate from these communities. Therefore, we do ensure that this investment's proceeds are reinvested in local firms. It's an ex-Wall Street employee's method of keeping "ten toes down" and conducting business in the Hussle fashion. If all goes according to plan, Gross' work could end up becoming one of Hussle's most enduring legacies. "I'm not doing this for the community," he claims. "I'm working on this with the neighbourhood.

Mother of Nipsey refuses to be sad for her kid. She would rather see his supporters honour his memory and spirit. She responded to a teacher who indicated her kids were upset by Hussle's passing: "I don't want you to be traumatised." "I want you to know that Ermias is right here with me right now and that I am very delighted. I sense him. My son now understands the key to life's mystery. Death is not anything to fear. You should mentally prepare for death. when one walks the earth and performs acts of kindness for others. Smith finds solace in her son's expression of contentment as he was being placed in his casket. "I murmured, 'That's my angel baby,' as I gazed upon him. He is a baby right now in the spirit world. Hussle's mother takes the time to console others in their sorrow while smiling. Please don't remain lying down. Do not weep. Because Nipsey has no boundaries and no constraints, he is now even better than before... Ermias won't pass away. In your heart, you have him. Ermias lives whenever you mention him. Dawit Asghedom made the statement immediately after Ermias was buried at Hollywood Hills' Forest Lawn Cemetery, also the ultimate resting place of Rodney King, John Singleton, Walt Disney, and Michael Jackson. "As a father, I wish my son was still here with me," Asghedom added. "But he did not die in vain, either. People are aware of what he intended to do and what, at just 33 years old, he has already accomplished.Nobody could have predicted how much he would be adored and supported by the public. Nothing can be explained with words. As we marched through the streets from the Marathon shop to the Staples Center. It was astounding.

Blacc Sam remarked, "We'll attempt to keep going as much as we can. Samantha, his sister, declares that Nipsey's legacy will endure. "Definitely. I have no doubts. I have no doubts.

As more people are motivated by Nipsey's example, councilmember Marqueece Harris-Dawson sees Nipsey's work expanding. I anticipate the Marathon shop, and more crucially, the Marathon store concept, will be successful, he claims. "I believe that because he has achieved financial success, others will start to follow his lead. People will travel to South Los Angeles, to the Crenshaw District, and to this neighbourhood to consume the culture produced there.

Nipsey was aware of the dangers of staying so accessible to his community. As a self-made millionaire, he was just as willing to take those risks as he had been when he was a young Slauson Boy. He admitted to me a year before his passing, "To be honest, that corner was known for robberies." "On that corner, there would be a lot of robberies. There is no longer any of that. In my entire community, there is a consensus that anyone who comes here is doing so to promote the community's welfare as a whole. Nipsey's death in front of the structure he built was his punishment for having faith in his community. That sacrifice will have been in naught if his effort is not carried forward. And that would be a tragedy on a whole new level. Hussle has handed the torch—or rather, several torches—to others. The Marathon must never end for that single justification.

Iddris Sandu responds, "Yeah, we're going to carry on his legacy." Every project he was engaged in. the STEM undertaking. Vector90. Towards Crenshaw. It was a documentary. All of it will continue to be done by us.He truly understood that it was not about him. Actually, it's for us. Hussle thought about his legacy during a 2018 Billboard interview. "I just want to have an impact on the next 12-year-old Nip Hussle," he declared. "I want to inspire the young men and women and impart the wisdom I've gained along the way. I'll inform them and reaffirm their naive impressions. I desire to be one of the voices or one of the narratives that asserts, "Nah, you're right." You are incredibly strong. Your capacity is the greatest... I want to be one of those people who does more than just say that; I want to be an example of it.

"I'm a Black man first," the Black LAPD officer declares. "I work with these guys every day if you want to know what the police department or police officers feel about Nipsey Hussle. They are not allowed to exalt gang members. The fact that the Black community cares about what he was doing, giving back, and helping doesn't matter. But they cannot permit a gang member to represent himself with that type of structure nearby. And because I am aware of my location, I repress my feelings in that regard. I am aware of my location to a T. When I work for the police, I'm not trying to come out here and carry a banner for Nipsey Hussle. He giving back is of no concern to them. He is a gang member to them, and that is all they will ever see him as.

Hussle reflected on his trip up to that point during his last visit to Big Boy's Neighborhood and encapsulated the tenacious spirit of the Marathon. He responded, "We were declined. Our failure. has failures. Frequently had to start from scratch. Yes, but we persisted in our efforts. It doesn't matter who you are; that's always what sets you apart. Obviously, the Marathon is the name of the company. It merely signifies endurance. It means to remain down.

If he had ever lost faith, Big Boy questioned. Have you ever thought, "Man, this ain't going to work"?

Hussle stated, "That's why I name my thing the Marathon. I won't pretend to have the perfect composure or act like I know what I'm doing. Nah. But I didn't give up. The only distinctive feature is that. I experienced every feeling. And I believe that's what will set apart those who attempt to pursue something: you won't give up. You're going to adopt the attitude of "I'm going to die in support of what I'm doing right now."

In keeping with that, Blacc Sam has committed to seeing the Nipsey Hussle Tower—a mixed-use residential structure that will eventually house affordable housing, a remodelled flagship location of The Marathon Clothing, and a Nipsey Hussle museum—completed.

Sam responded to the Los Angeles city attorney's efforts to close down The Marathon Clothing business with a statement that read, "Nipsey was a true inspiration for the have nots." "He was a champion of the people. He overcame all odds and succeeded. He flourished in uncertain circumstances. In the streets, he was completely respected. His sense of honour and responsibility served as his moral compass at all times because he "led" by example....

No matter what attempts are made to prevent it, Nipsey's ambition will be realised and handed down to his progeny. The Nipsey Hussle Tower will motivate people and demonstrate that, despite starting from nothing, anyone can succeed. The narrative of Nipsey Hussle will be recorded in history. The Nipsey Hussle tower will be constructed, and his legacy will live on forever in both stone and people's hearts.

On Slauson Avenue, it is early afternoon. The enormous Nipsey Hussle paintings in the alleyway by the Fatburger connecting Slauson Avenue to Fifty-Eighth Place are attracting throngs of tourists who want to take photographs against them. The aptly titled Shitty Cuz rushed through this alley on March 31, 2019, holding two weapons in each hand and wearing a hood over his chest. It will probably go on for all time whether Eric Holder acted alone out of envious wrath, was prodded by the hood, or was recruited by the cops. The defeat is still the same in the end. Neighborhood Nip's murder was a crime against humanity.

The grandmother of rapper Hussle says, "I'm praying for him too." "I sincerely hope he is not killed while being held. He has enough time to repent and seek God's pardon. Being Catholic, I do think in praying, therefore I'm praying for him right now. He was inexperienced and young, so I hope he regrets what he did.

Few people are as affected by the loss as Slauson Bruce. When Hussle originally recruited him to begin cleaning the parking lot, he was in a desperate situation. Bruce is resting on a small red concrete wall outside the locked chain-link fence that now completely encloses the parking lot at 3420 West Slauson Ave, which was previously the location of a thriving centre of commerce, the Marathon Clothing smart store, as he waits for a business meeting today. There is a shopping cart full of miscellaneous items next to Bruce. Bruce makes time to speak, donning an Adidas tracksuit and a battered black fedora.

I worked hard, adds Bruce. "Man, I constructed this place. I'll tell you that. This lot was once steam cleaned by me. Kind of trash. Window cleaning. Really, it's just me. Nipsey wouldn't be here, though. At the studio, he would be. Sam, his brother, Fatts, and they would be in control while he was gone. Bruce begins by coughing violently. He declared that he wouldn't have time for that. He was forced to write songs.

When Bruce first encountered Nipsey, he was collecting cans while riding his bike. He recalls the moment that changed his life vividly and answers, "Fifteen long years ago. "He backed out of the driveway and thought I was in the way."

The door was opened by Nipsey.

"You all right?" he enquired.

I replied, "Yeah. I need employment.

Nipsey informed him, "You keep this lot clean, you got one." In 2004, Nipsey Hussle's name was little recognized outside of the Crenshaw District. Bruce Slauson claims to have been present ever since. He responds, "You damn right," when asked if he could tell Hussle was unique.

Hussle recognized something in Bruce as well, and they grew close. Bruce remembers, "So we talked and talked and talked." He then declared, "Wait a minute, I'm going to put you in a movie!" As promised, Nipsey hired Slauson Bruce to play the lead role in "The Midas Touch," a YouTube video that was released as part of the Victory Lap album launch on February 1, 2018. Bruce gets into Nipsey's Maybach in the ten-minute film after leaving the shopping cart behind. Bruce purchases a charcoal-grey suit from Tom Ford in Beverly Hills and a new haircut at the Shave Parlor on Slauson and Seventh Avenue. He visits a jewellery store to purchase a gold ring, watch, bracelet, and chain before receiving a massage and mani-pedi. Following a lobster dinner with part of the All Money In team and getting all swagged up, Bruce visits a posh strip club.

Ever after March 31, everything has changed. Since then, it hasn't been great, says Bruce. "I can't fall asleep at night." Pet Bull, his dog, looks at him, and Bruce reciprocates. He says, "I start crying every night." "However, I replied there is nothing I can do about it. He was parking and leaving when he said, "The Marathon continues," according to what he said to me before he passed away. I vowed to see it that way.Because of all that he accomplished for us.

On the day Nipsey was killed, Bruce had cleaned up the parking lot. He continues, his voice a little softer than before, "I had just left." I don't stay around here. I used to hang out and everything at first, but as time went on, I stopped. To clean up the lot, I would arrive at six. I was then employed by Woody's. After that, I would clean up somewhere else at night. Oh man, three jobs a day.

All of those positions are now vacant. Two years ago, Bruce's girlfriend passed away while sleeping. He says, "I've been going through all kinds of crap." Since then, he has somewhat lost the Marathon's momentum. He says, turning to face Crenshaw up Slauson Avenue, "I ain't doing' nothing." "I have no luck," you say. However, he thinks Blacc Sam will restore this location. It's gated because of that, Bruce says. They are constructing apartments there.

Just then, a woman on foot crosses the street from the opposite direction. A few blocks away, she claims to have spotted Nipsey's godbrother Adam.

"Where?"

"There," as in "at the place."

The question "Talk to him?"

This time, "not." Without saying another word, she hands Bruce some cash and then turns around to head back the way she came. The hustle is constant.

"That was my sister just now," Bruce says. From Chicago, she brought several orders. Her companion placed a shirt order. Even online ordering is not possible for them. They retreated. You won't find any.

Hey, man, the Marathon continues, if Bruce could say anything to Nipsey right now, it would be that. You better believe it."

It does, in fact, go on. even if everything is hidden from view by the locked gate, the barbed wire, and the thick green cloth. To deter unauthorised visitors from loitering in the parking area where the Marathon Clothing store still remains, a barrier was erected on August 1, 2019. The cops are constantly on the lookout for mistakes that could harm Nipsey's team. Fans of Nipsey continue to come out every day, unfazed. Well-wishers from all over the world have gathered here in the months after his death, taking pictures, praying, and writing innumerable messages—RIP Nip, TMC 4Ever, Hussle The Great!—on every available square inch of wall and window space.

This commercial centre at 3420 West Slauson Ave is now sacred land, just as significant to Nipsey, Sam, Adam, and Fatts as it was in their earlier years. A prophet's blood was shed here, and there is no fence high enough to contain the love. The world knows that Nipsey Hussle is the people's champion, but the Los Angeles City Attorney's Office doesn't seem to agree.

Sam excitedly exclaimed, "We bought the lot, man," at his brother's memorial service on April 11 at the Staples Center. "I'm not sure how we managed it. And considering that he used to peddle CDs out of the trunk, that was a major deal for him, man. You all know what we went through with the cops in that parking lot when he used to be there, and they used to try to eject him from the lot.

Throughout the years he worked for the family firm, Bruce frequently saw the dispute. "Sam told me—what did he say? The police came and tore the property down. The big retribution, oh my. He constructed this thing in just two days. "They won't stop me," What he said was that. Everything is also lawful. They weren't dispensing any drugs. They are attempting to search for weapons and other crap. They didn't bear that trash, those boys. They were acting legally. Conspiracy theories do not hold Bruce's attention. If you ask him who killed Nipsey, he will tell you straight up: "What you call a hater," he responds. "You motherfucker is jealous. That is my opinion. What about the fact that Hussle allegedly knew him, though? It's possible that your best friend is an envious motherfucker.

Blacc Sam has persisted in fighting in court for his family's rights and to uphold his brother's legacy. Less than two months after Hussle's passing, on May 16, the company Crips LLC submitted trademark applications, including one for the right to use Hussle's tagline "The Marathon Continues" on clothes. On May 28, Sam submitted a similar trademark application. A Crips LLC representative apologised after Sam made his public remarks in July 2019. The organisation acknowledged that the application may have been "offensive," and that they had contacted the family, the statement read. "There will absolutely be no trademark legal battle between their organisation and Blacc Sam, brother of the late Nipsey Hussle." But words are often overshadowed by deeds. Nipsey Hussle's estate filed a lawsuit in October 2020, asking for monetary damages as well as a court order compelling the business to remove any unlawful Marathon items since Crips LLC had not abandoned its application.

In 2013, shortly after producing 100 racks in a single evening at the inaugural Crenshaw pop-up store, Hussle spoke with Complex about the reasons behind Nipsey Hussle fans' deep affinity. Why? "Because I'm real, my nigga," he replied. "My tale is true. There are no other rappers like me in the industry at all. particularly those of my generation. No nigga has ever confronted what I have confronted. experienced what I experienced. thought in my way. never gave up. stayed in the shit and remained seated. built for his neighbourhood. influenced his community by remaining local. came from the Rollin' 60s, a dangerous time period. went head-to-head and toe-to-toe with killers. No nigga in the game compares to me. So that's what they're responding to, along with the fact that I use my music to speak my truth. Reverend Abdullah, a well-groomed young brother wearing a sharp suit and tie, is down the block from Slauson Bruce hawking copies of The Final Call, the Nation of Islam publication. The cover story for the newspaper's April 9, 2019, issue was titled "The Life, Loss, and Legacy of Nipsey Hussle." 100,000 copies of that issue were distributed by the NOI throughout Los Angeles during the week leading up to Hussle's funeral. At the Staples Center for Hussle's memorial service, which was broadcast nationwide, Minister Louis Farrakhan stated Nipsey "is to hip-hop and rap what Bob Marley was to reggae; he is the prophetic voice of all in that community." (Stephen Marley, Bob's son, responded to a question about Hussle's death by saying, "Even though we didn't know him, it was a sad moment for everyone. Everyone was affected.

Reverend Abdullah claims that neither he nor his brother ever refused the paper. "Never refused."

Reverend Abdullah believes that the tragedy of March 31st, 2019 may have had a beneficial effect because it brought attention to the Crenshaw District and the work Hussle was doing there. "Definitely a bad situation. However, people are more conscious of what is going on in the neighbourhood. Not that the death of the brother is a good thing. The fact that so many people are aware of what he was doing, what his message was, and what the issues are, however, is positive. Long before Hussle passed away, Reverend Abdullah was selling the newspaper at the retail centre on Slauson and Crenshaw. "Absolutely," he replies. He saw a familiar face. Several chats had. seen one another at various locations. I wanted to conduct an interview since I genuinely did love him for this reason. Hell yes.

He still recalls their initial encounter. Pointing to the parking lot, he continues, "It was right over there." It was simply astounding how personable he was and that he actually lived his message out in the streets. He wasn't one of those rappers who makes up stories or, you know, a way of life. He had a shoebox full of money when I first met him. He took a break from counting the shoebox to buy a newspaper, then he started counting again. I'm not sure what the transaction was, but he certainly fit that description of a person. I only want the world to be aware of that. What lesson will be learned from his experience? Reverend Abdullah: "I think people should keep giving back." I believe that people should just learn. I can't share my lesson with you. I learned countless lessons from it. It's similar to certain books. You'll have to read it to find out what it means; I can't tell you. However, make sure you support the neighbourhood. Continue to do it. carry on from where he left off. The book Message to the Blackman in America was given to T.I. continue from where he left off.

He would say, "I love you," if he could only say one thing to Hussle. I cherish you, bro. I'm done now. Without a doubt. I appreciate it, Nipsey Hussle.

The contents of this book may not be copied, reproduced or transmitted without the express written permission of the author or publisher. Under no circumstances will the publisher or author be responsible or liable for any damages, compensation or monetary loss arising from the information contained in this book, whether directly or indirectly. .

Disclaimer Notice:

Although the author and publisher have made every effort to ensure the accuracy and completeness of the content, they do not, however, make any representations or warranties as to the accuracy, completeness, or reliability of the content. , suitability or availability of the information, products, services or related graphics contained in the book for any purpose. Readers are solely responsible for their use of the information contained in this book

Every effort has been made to make this book possible. If any omission or error has occurred unintentionally, the author and publisher will be happy to acknowledge it in upcoming versions.

Made in United States
Troutdale, OR
05/04/2025